Sandtray Applications to Trauma Therapy

T0384998

Sandtray Applications to Trauma Therapy presents the theory behind and the practicalities of using sandtray therapy in treatment with traumatized patients, both children and adults.

The book begins with a review of the most frequently asked questions that professionals ask themselves when using the sandtray. It then details the Barudy and Dantagnan model of trauma therapy to understand and integrate sandtray therapy with patients who have suffered trauma. Chapters describe the importance of neuroaffective communication, directive and non-directive working methodologies and how to use the technique in regulation, empowerment, and resilient integration of trauma. A featured chapter by the second author, Dr Raffael Benito, presents the neurobiology behind sandtray therapy, outlining step by step what happens in the brain of a patient during a sandtray session. Transcripts of clinical cases, sandtray images and true client stories are integrated throughout.

This practical volume will appeal to sandtray practitioners, trauma therapists, psychologists and psychiatrists working with patient experiences of abandonment, mistreatment or sexual abuse, among others.

José Luis Gonzalo Marrodán, PhD, is a psychologist specialist in clinical psychology, psychotherapist by the EFPA, postgraduate in systemic-infant trauma therapy by the IFIV of Barcelona and clinical EMDR specialist for adults. Since 1999 his field of professional interest has focused on attachment-based psychotherapy and trauma therapy with adopted and foster children and youth in his private clinic. He runs a blog: www.buenostratos.com.

Rafael Benito Moraga, PhD, is a psychiatrist, family therapist and postgraduate in systemic-child trauma therapy by the IFIV of Barcelona. He works in his private clinic conducting psychiatric and psychotherapeutic treatment of adolescents and adults. Since 1999, his field of professional interest has focused on the impact of adverse circumstances suffered in childhood on neurobiological and physiological development throughout life.

"A wonderful book that will illuminate practitioners in their task of helping young people understand and overcome their traumatic experiences, build resilience and progress through a healthier, long-term developmental path. The book is rooted in a secure base of more than one hundred years of child and adolescent mental health, from which it explores and digs deeply into the therapeutic applications of the sandtray technique, whilst integrating the domains of trauma, resilience, parental skills, and neuroscience, within a framework of attachment-based thinking and practice."

Arturo Ezquerro is a London-based consultant psychiatrist, psychoanalytic psychotherapist, and group analyst.

"The risk is that upon discovering the existence of therapeutic techniques as attractive and promising as the sandtray, they are applied with the illusion that these by themselves will be sufficient, neglecting the care that should be taken to apply, contextualize and integrate them in a process that is relational, affectively binding, empathic and mentalizing between therapist and patient. Thanks to their human quality, their extensive training and their rich clinical experience, the authors have the skills and sufficient authority to affirm that Traumatherapy is the ideal scenario that guarantees the effective and respectful application of the sandtray technique, applying it in the moment and adapting it to the uniqueness of each child or adolescent."

Jorge Barudy is a neuropsychiatrist, psychotherapist, family therapist, and trainer of the EFTA (European Association of Family Therapy).
Maryorie Dantagnan is a pedagogue, psychologist, child psychotherapist and co-director of IFIV, Spain.

Sandtray Applications to Trauma Therapy

A Model Towards Relational Harmony

José Luis Gonzalo Marrodán and Rafael Benito Moraga

Routledge
Taylor & Francis Group

LONDON AND NEW YORK

First published 2024
by Routledge
4 Park Square, Milton Park, Abingdon, Oxon OX14 4RN

and by Routledge
605 Third Avenue, New York, NY 10158

Routledge is an imprint of the Taylor & Francis Group, an informa business

© 2024 José Luis Gonzalo Marrodán and Rafael Benito Moraga

Designed cover image: © Getty Images

British Library Cataloguing in Publication Data
A catalogue record for this book is available from the British Library

Library of Congress Cataloging-in-Publication Data
Library of Congress Cataloging-in-Publication Data
Names: Gonzalo Marrodán, José Luis, 1967- author. | Benito Moraga, Rafael, 1964- author.
Title: Sandtray applications to trauma therapy : a model towards relational harmony / José Luis Gonzalo Marrodán and Rafael Benito Moraga.
| Includes bibliographical references and index. | communication, directive and non-Identifiers: LCCN 2023005115 (print) | LCCN 2023005116 (ebook) |
Subjects: LCSH: Sandplay—Therapeutic use. | Play therapy. | Psychic trauma—Treatment.
Classification: LCC RC489.S25 G66 2024 (print) | LCC RC489.S25 (ebook) | DDC 616.89/1653–dc23/eng/20230522
LC record available at https://lccn.loc.gov/2023005115
LC ebook record available at https://lccn.loc.gov/2023005116
A catalog record has been requested for this book

ISBN: 978-1-032-41660-1 (hbk)
ISBN: 978-1-032-41657-1 (pbk)
ISBN: 978-1-003-35911-1 (ebk)

DOI: 10.4324/9781003359111

Typeset in Times New Roman
by Taylor & Francis Books

Contents

Illustrations

Figures

Tables

Acknowledgements

To all our relatives and friends, because it's through the bond that unites us that we find the meaning and emotional nourishment needed to undertake our work with passion and live fully.

To our professors and friends Jorge Barudy and Maryorie Dantagnan for reading the manuscript, for the suggestions provided and for the excellent prologue they have given us. After training with you, we now have the honour of sharing an exciting project: teaching in the Postgraduate course in Child-systemic Trauma therapy.

Our gratitude to the psychologist and professor Josefina Martínez for teaching us to work with the sandtray technique within the Postgraduate course in child-systemic trauma therapy during the unforgettable summer of 2006 in Barcelona. Josefina Martínez works at the Metáfora Center in Santiago de Chile, where she teaches a course in play psychotherapy which also includes sandtray training. Her website is http://terapiadejuego.cl

To our friend Dr Arturo Ezquerro for supporting our work, reading the original manuscript and giving us a beautiful prologue.

To all our patients, because it's with them that every day that we learn to be better professionals and, above all, people. Our thoughts are with you creating this book and in our daily work to help you on your path of emotional healing.

To all the students of the sandtray workshops for sharing all the wonderful experiences of emotional and relational harmony while training with the technique.

Preface

Jorge Barudy and Maryorie Dantagnan

Like all human productions, this book, whose author asked us to preface, is part of a story. As in all stories, there are multiple characters that make up the plot. We are part of it, but the main characters are José Luis Gonzalo, the main protagonist, and Rafael Benito, who gifted this work a magnificent chapter.

As part of this story and authors of the prologue, we have taken advantage of this space to tell you how our paths crossed with those of the authors. To do so, we will begin with a bit of our own story.

It was the last months of the year 1998. When the year 2000 was announced on the horizon, we received a beautiful and meaningful gift from life: our professional paths crossed in Temuco, a southern city in Chile and a very meaningful place for us. Our meeting gave birth to a couple united by those multiple and luminous feelings that make up love, which in turn enriched our professional practices.

As a pedagogue, psychologist and child psychotherapist working in social programmes in Colombia, Maryorie knew the traumatic impact of the unjust, cowardly and violent living conditions of hundreds of Colombian boys and girls. As a result of her therapeutic practice with children living in poor and outcast environments, she became aware of how these contexts played a fundamental role in generating suffering and psychological disorders in children. When widowed, she returned to her country of origin, Chile, putting her knowledge and clinical experience at the service of children who were living in a similar environment and affected by different types of abuse in their families.

As a neuropsychiatrist, child psychiatrist and family therapist who had trained in Belgium after his exile, Jorge learned the invisible pain of those children who grew up in violent environments on account of adults. He was professionally involved in programmes aimed at the therapeutic repair of children's wounds caused by organised violence—wars, political repression, persecution, sexism, religion—as well as those caused by domestic child abuse.

Our meeting allowed us to quickly realise that we agreed on the need to contribute to the design of a therapeutic methodology adapted to child suffering as a result of traumatic experiences and adult abuse from family, institutions and society.

What emerged from our rich conversations was that we had to strive not only to criticise and denounce the fact that most psychotherapeutic treatments for children with mental health problems do not take into account the suffering and damage caused by adult abuse, but also that we had to pair up to investigate and propose an alternative methodology.

For us, it was evident that adult action, or lack thereof—a lot of which significant—made children and young people express their suffering through disorders; including those invisible cases that occurred in families of favoured classes, often camouflaged by classist social representations and/or violent educational conceptions.

What seemed most worrying to us is that at a social level and on many occasions in the professional environment, violence and abuse in families, schools, institutions or in society weren't considered at all when investigating the origin of the so-called "child and adolescent psychopathological disorders". In these contexts, adults mistreat, abuse and/or neglect children, owing to incompetence, beliefs or unresolved traumatic experiences. What was most painful for us were the multiple situations in which parents abused their children as a result of what they had suffered in their own childhood, but whose suffering hadn't been acknowledged.

Our clinical work with children and their families allowed us to convert our pain and indignation for these transgenerational injustices into active research. This gave life to the therapeutic methodology that we call systemic infant-juvenile trauma therapy, mentioned and extensively treated by the author of this book.

This active research that we began in 1999 included and includes applying the methodology of participant observation to detect how traumatic experiences affected children, emphasising comprehensive observation and, at the same time, employing instruments and therapeutic techniques accordingly.

Our comprehensive observation was first of all influenced by what we had learned in our respective trainings: Maryorie's psychodynamic approach, focused on the attachment paradigm, and Jorge's psychiatric training, redefined with the contributions of the humanist psychological current (Carl Rogers), epistemology and the systemic paradigm, which he had the opportunity to teach at the Catholic University of Louvain in Belgium. Our formations nourished our vision of the world and of society, but we won't stop insisting that suffering of children is also a result of the injustices created by economic and social inequalities, as well as abusive cultures derived from patriarchal conceptions, from savage neo-liberalism to the religious conceptions that endorse violence against women and children.

Our knowledge has been nourished by multiple contributions from research related to attachment, trauma psychology, developmental psychology, self-organisation stages; all of this having the contributions of relational neuroscience as its foundations, which have revolutionised our knowledge on the way our brain works and the human mind.

The contributions of the investigations of the new disciplines known as epigenetics and molecular biology have given us the last gifts: they have allowed us to validate our hypotheses, to the extent that what is being discovered confirms many of the fundamentals of our approach.

These contributions, together with our systematised clinical observations, gave rise to what we call the Comprehensive Assessment Guideline for child suffering that aims to encompass the most relevant aspects of the impact of child and adolescent abuse. In this sense, this guideline is the basis which supports our intervention model: systemic child and adolescent trauma therapy, whose foundation is our paradigm of Good Treatment of Children. When the abuse is within the family, our methodology considers the evaluation of parental skills and parental resilience to be essential. In this sense, the promotion of child, family and parental resilience is a cross purpose of all our therapeutic interventions.

Our professional practices have enabled us to provide therapeutic support to many children and adolescents affected by different contexts of violence and neglect. We know their pain caused by abuse in their families, but also by institutions, including those intended for protection. We have also been learning how to provide therapeutic support to hundreds of boys and girls affected by the violence of wars, exile, as well as the indolence of the rulers of rich countries who deny them shelter and solidarity. These boys and girls have shown us their wounds, but also their resilience, as well as the courage of their mothers and fathers, taking them to safer places and saving them from death. We have also been applying our trauma therapy methodology for more than ten years to treat the early traumas of adopted sons and daughters in different regions of the world.

Traumatherapy was born from its start in our therapeutic work with children and adolescents. The application of its neurosequential principle, as well as its epistemological foundations, has allowed us to gradually adapt it to adult patients currently affected by trauma as a result of torture, war, exile and male chauvinist conjugal violence; traumas that often build up on others experienced during childhood.

The birth of a diploma: meeting José Luis Gonzalo and Rafael Benito

As a logical result of our learning and after having designed and applied the first bases of our work methodology with children, we feel the need to share what we have learned. This is because we had noticed considerable improvements in the children and adolescents cared for in our programme, within our NGO EXIL in Barcelona. We had compared our perceptions with the beneficiaries of the Programme and with the systematic observation of their educators. The first group of participants in our programme was made up of boys, girls and young people affected by experiences of severe abuse, for which they had been given protection through reception centres in Barcelona. Later, we were able to employ Traumatherapy[1] with children and adolescents from the foster homes and residences belonging to the COTS Foundation of the city of Manresa, in Catalonia. Both the directors of the Foundation, the teams of educators in the various houses, as well as the reference educators designated as tutors of the boys and girls, have actively participated by playing the role of co-therapists, as we call it in our model.

The conditions illustrated here explain our decision to propose a post-graduate training programme that we titled Diploma in Systemic Childhood Traumatherapy in 2004. From the beginning, we carried out our training project based on three axes: sharing a comprehensive model of the suffering and disorders shown in boys and girls as an expression of the traumas resulting from the abuse they had suffered; secondly, sharing the techniques that we were applying; and thirdly, offering the candidates the opportunity to work on themselves through the relationship with the therapist.

Thanks to this project we had the opportunity to meet José Luis Gonzalo, the author of this book, and Rafael Benito, whose contribution to this work is invaluable. They were part of that first group of professionals who trusted us by participating in the training; outstanding professionals like many from that first promotion, who get the credit for having helped us to make our training project possible. Just like sons daughters give their parents the opportunity to be mothers or fathers, this group turned us into therapist trauma trainers. They get all the credit for contributing with their own knowledge, as a result of their clinical experiences and their eagerness to investigate the work of many authors, experts in the treatment of childhood traumas, ideas and instruments to improve their practices; and for having contributed to enrich our methodology from the beginning. For this reason, prologuing this work is a way of thanking them for their contributions, their generosity in daily sharing and for having accepted—as of 2009—to join our training activities, first collaborating with our programme in Barcelona and then actively working as teachers and presenters of the training programme that takes place in the Basque Country.

In our Diploma we share and teach childhood professionals from communities throughout the Spanish State, as well as from our country of origin, Chile. Our therapeutic methodology is based on a systemic reading of child suffering and an integrating paradigm whose main domains are attachment, trauma, development, parental skills and resilience.

What we share with the participants is the systemic trauma therapy model, which consists of animating a therapeutic process that prioritises an individual systemic intervention, organised in three blocks of work featuring support, accompaniment and promotion of the patient's parenting skills, or co-therapist in this model (educators of reception centres, foster parents or adoptive parents). Therefore, attachment, attuned response and coherent and consistent responses or interventions towards the child are the key elements to work on.

As we have mentioned, this model of **Systemic Infant Juvenile Trau-matherapy** is made up of three blocks: Block I, whose purpose is *Tuning and self-regulation*; Block II to facilitate *Empowerment* and Block III, to accompany the *Resilient Reintegration* of traumatic experiences. Addressing a detailed description of these three blocks is beyond the purpose of this prologue. As the author deals with these contents in a dynamic and illustrative way, we will limit ourselves to listing them, insisting on their fundamentals.

Block I aims to ensure that children or adolescents learn about a relationship akin to that between a sufficiently competent mother and her offspring, to develop an experience of secure attachment. This is challenging because in most cases, complex, cumulative and early traumatic experiences have forced children or young people to develop models of insecure or disorganised attachments, which are the manifestation of fear and mistrust in relationships with adults. Therefore, to achieve the purpose of this block, the therapist must interact and communicate in an affective, empathetic (attuned and resonant) and mentalising way. This will favour the ability of the child or adolescent to self-regulate their internal states, which are seriously deregulated as a consequence of the disorganisation of their mental states caused by suffering, pain and stress responses to morbid stressors that are often unthinkable.

Learning about and applying the sandtray technique, which is widely illustrated in this book, we discovered a very useful instrument to achieve the purpose of Block I, because its application allows the child or adolescent to develop or strengthen their self-observation, with less resistance. This allows a better understanding of one's internal states, by gradually managing to identify, express and modulate one's emotions. The sandtray technique applied as proposed in this book, allows to reinforce an affective, empathetic and mentalising communication between the therapist and the children and adolescents and therefore helps them to gradually approach the experience of secure attachment. But let's also remember that tuning has a multidirectional dimension already discussed in this book.

Block II is aimed at the empowerment and active participation of children or young people in the therapeutic process. Helping them in this is essential: as we often say, the essence of trauma is the feeling of absolute helplessness and following the path of empowerment is the only way to counteract this.

What we created in our practice and what has been proposed by several other authors has inspired us to contribute to this block with various techniques that aim to give back to the patients the power to direct their lives, taken away by the adults who have mistreated and abused.

Block III aims at the resilient reintegration of the contents of the traumatic experiences, in order to facilitate a new integration, different from past experiences. Giving a new meaning to what the patients went through allows them to employ their energies and resources to the fullest to overcome the impact of the damage, but also motivates them not to repeat what has happened to them in their present or future interpersonal relationships, e.g., with their children, in your life as a couple or other relationships. The resignification of the cause and effects of traumatic experiences opens the door to the extraordinary phenomenon called Resilience.

José Luis Gonzalo and Rafael Benito also masterfully present the role of the sandtray methodology in meeting the objectives of this block.

The pleasure and pride of making the prologue of this book

We want to conclude this prologue by expressing the pleasure and pride we have felt reading José Luis Gonzalo and Rafael Benito. This book is the result of two learning processes we feel part of. In it, two aspects are intertwined: the observations made by José Luis Gonzalo, collected after his training in 2004 and having applied Systemic Infant Juvenile Traumatherapy with children and adolescents for over 20 years, as well as with adults affected by complex and cumulative trauma; and then those that emerge from the systematic application of the sandtray technique with their patients. We are convinced that José Luis Gonzalo is one of the most experienced psychotherapist psychologists in the Hispanic world, with his rigorous and systematic application of the sandtray technique with traumatised patients. He is also one of the professionals whose excellent training in child and adolescent psychotraumatology has allowed him to make valuable contributions to interventions and ways of working in this technique, such as the registration guidelines and the intervention guidelines.

As for Rafael Benito, a psychiatrist and trauma therapist who honours his profession for his courage in confronting the dominant thought in his specialty. What he brings to this book is what the dominant currents call child-juvenile psychopathology, which can be treated in a more adequate and coherent way when considering his biographical framework. Not only have his contributions helped us understand the impact of traumatherapy and the sandtray technique at a neurobiological level, but he has also masterfully described the therapeutic value of the methodology and the technique.

This book has the enormous merit of conceiving the sandtray technique as an instrument of great value for therapeutic work. We insist that an instrument like this cannot be decontextualised from a therapeutic process, i.e., a technique doesn't make the process. José Luis Gonzalo states this and it is reflected in all his work: the application is describing with examples, which is a technique, not the process. This can be dealt with at different moments of the process, accompanying and facilitating the creation carried out by the patients block by block, step by step, but this application does not replace the integral process of traumatherapy organised in three blocks. This is a fundamental contribution to prevent some of the most dangerous mistakes that many therapists make, as a result of their lack of experience or under the pressure of the dominant ideology focused on the application of easy, economic solutions. When techniques are sold as therapeutic processes, the illusion of a pseudo-effectiveness emerges, which only aggravates the suffering and damage that adults have caused to many children and adolescents. A therapeutic process such as traumatherapy is highly complex, which implies using many techniques in a coherent, responsible and creative way. The risk is that upon discovering the existence of therapeutic techniques as attractive and promising as the sandtray, they are applied with the illusion that these by themselves will be sufficient, neglecting the care that should be taken to apply, contextualise and integrate them in a process that is relational, affectively binding, empathic and mentalising between therapist and patient. Thanks to his human quality, his extensive training and his rich clinical experience, the author has the skills and sufficient authority to affirm that Traumatherapy is the ideal scenario that guarantees the effective and respectful application of the sandtray technique, applying it in the moment and adapting it to the uniqueness of each child or adolescent. The organisation of the contents to work on in each block, following the neurosequential principle, is the best guarantee so that the therapeutic impact of using the sandtray keeps all its meaning and effectiveness.

Lastly, the richness of the examples that didactically illustrate the processes described is an invaluable help for any therapist who is captivated by this technique -or even more by the technique itself, fascinated by that wounded boy, girl, adolescent, woman or man who gives the therapist the space and the opportunity to explore and feel what he has created together with his patient. All the examples described reflect a fundamental principle that must be present in the work of every therapist: "*We prioritise the therapeutic relationship over the content to interpret, whatever the technique we use.*" All this work is a beautiful example of this.

Jorge Barudy is a neuropsychiatrist, psychotherapist and family therapist. Trainer of the EFTA (European Association of Family Therapy). Professor of the postgraduate course in psychotherapy and systemic social intervention at the Catholic University of Louvain (1983–98). He was Clinical Director of the programme for the prevention and treatment of child abuse (Equipe SOS Enfants Familles) at the Catholic University of Leuven, Belgium (1982–97). Founding Director of EXIL Brussels in 1983, Psychosocial Medical Center for political refugees and victims of torture in Belgium and since 2000 Director and President of the Exil Center (Psychosocial Medical Association for victims of violence, torture and violation of Human Rights) in Barcelona, Spain. Professor of several Spanish, European and Latin American Universities in post-graduate courses in relation to the prevention and treatment of the effects of violence on children, women, the family and the community.

He is Co-Director of IFIV Barcelona, founded in 2000. Author of numerous articles and books on the subject of child abuse, good treatment, parental competence and resilience.

Maryorie Dantagnan is a pedagogue, psychologist and child psychotherapist. He has been responsible for programmes to promote children's mental health and the prevention of child abuse in Barranquilla, Colombia. Co-ordinator of the children's team of the Apega Barcelona centre and of the psychotherapy programme for children who are victims of abuse at the EXIL Spain centre. Teacher and trainer in Spain, France, Belgium and Chile in different post-graduate courses, both in training activities of the public or private adminis-tration, as well as in the field of education. Co-director of IFIV, author of different articles and manuals on abused childhood and parenting. Co-author of the books *Good treatment of childhood: parenting, attachment and resi-lience, The invisible challenges of being a parent. Handbook for assessing par-enting skills and resilience, The magical and realistic festival of children's resilience, Promoting parenting skills and resilience: Supporting women who have survived violence in their role as mothers* and *Maternal intelligence.*

1 ©The Systemic Childhood Traumatherapy of Barudy and Dantagnan is a registered trademark in the register of intellectual property.

Prologue

Arturo Ezquerro

Sandtray Applications to Traumatherapy: A Model Towards Relational Harmony, by José Luis Gonzalo and Rafael Benito, two seasoned clinicians, is a wonderful book that will illuminate practitioners, particularly those working with traumatised children and adolescents, in their task of helping these young people understand and overcome their traumatic experiences, build resilience and progress through a healthier, long-term developmental path in their lives.

It is widely accepted that the technique of sandtray therapy was originally employed by Dr Margaret Lowenfeld, a British paediatrician who, in the late 1920s, shifted her professional interest from practising medicine to exploring the newly born field of child psychotherapy. In the early 1930s she introduced a novel method in which she used two zinc trays in the children's playroom.

The first tray was half-filled with sand; the second contained water and a variety of objects used for shaping or moulding sand. A wonder box or *caja mágica*, filled with small toys, paper, pieces of metal and other colourful ornaments, was kept in close proximity to the trays (Friedman and Mitchell, 1994).

Dr Lowenfeld often reported that, over time, a significant proportion of the children she was treating referred to the wonder box as their *world*. That usually happened after they had created three-dimensional scenes, by combining elements from the box with the sand in the tray. This discovery prompted her to also describe her therapeutic approach as "the world technique".

It served as a means of communication between the patient (a scene builder) and the psychotherapist (an observer) giving the latter powerful insights into the former's internal world and whereabouts (Dale and Lyddon, 2000). Interestingly, Dr Lowenfeld seemed to have developed the idea of using sand trays in therapy after she read *Floor Games*, a book written by Herbert George Wells in 1911.

Wells was a prolific English writer, broadly considered the "father" of science fiction, who mastered many genres, including more than fifty novels and dozens of short stories. His work also encompassed non-fiction activities such as socio-political commentary and analysis, satire, popular science, history and other disciplines.

Remarkably, in *Floor Games*, Wells described nothing of his ongoing professional activities, but a number of fun-filled games that he and his sons played together on the floor, in the family home. Subsequently, Wells became very keen on encouraging play as a means of healthy psychosocial and personal development for children and their parents!

There was a wider context to the emergence of sandtray therapy. In 1911 the Romanian-born psychiatrist Jacob Moreno developed a technique of puppetry and drama in a child guidance clinic in Vienna, which he called *psychodrama* (Moreno, 1946).

Soon after, the Austrian psychiatrist and psychoanalyst Alfred Adler, who had departed from Sigmund Freud's inner circle, undertook his own independent research on human development. In the 1920s Adler further contributed to the expansion of child guidance clinics and emphasised that responsibility for the optimal development of the child is not limited to the parents but must also include teachers and society more broadly. In his model, children were allowed to act spontaneously in order to facilitate the expression of feelings, fantasies and conflicts.

In the 1940s Samuel Slavson proposed a technique in which the activity needs of children could be exploited for therapeutic gains. His technique came to be known as *activity group therapy*, which took full therapeutic advantage of the natural drive of children for playful action (Slavson and Schiffer, 1975).

Encouraging spontaneity may sometimes lead to the expression of aggressive feelings in both boys and girls. In the more severe cases of aggression, this was linked to past experiences in which the child had been the direct recipient of trauma, through abuse, aggression or exposure to witnessing it (Bowlby, 1938, 1939).

In the late 1940s a similar technique called *group play therapy* was developed by the American psychologist Virginia Axline (1950).

This was expanded by the Israeli teacher and child psychologist Haim Ginott (1961) in the following decade and has continued growing until the present time.

These practitioners incorporated some of the strategies of individual child analysis; they used play as a developmentally natural tool for the communication of thoughts, wishes, fears and other difficult feelings. It proved to be particularly useful a technique with the younger children, as their verbal-expression abilities are not entirely developed.

Playfulness is key to any meaningful therapeutic relationship with children, anyway. It may take the form of socio-dramatic play, an enactment of traumatic experiences or a playful approach to the world of the adult.

During the years I worked as a consultant child and adolescent psychiatrist, I learned that to carry out any sort of therapy with children involves having a capacity to talk to them (Ezquerro, 2017a).

Talking to children entails effort and practice. It is more difficult to talk therapeutically to children than to adults, because it requires a radical change in one's normal talking habits. Since most adult communications to children take the form of passing information, giving advice or dictating prohibition, they are largely one-way channels allowing for minimal feedback.

To establish a two-way communicative process with the child may demand from the adult a change of attitude and behaviour, as well as language.

The therapist must become interested in what the child has to say, which may represent an unusual viewpoint of the world, seen through innocent eyes. Relating to a child without talking down to him or her is not an easy task for many adults. Successful talking with children, above all, implies reciprocal communication.

It is vital that therapists working with children and adolescents make themselves sufficiently conversant with the developmental phases of childhood and adolescence, including the sequential changes that occur in the neuronal, cognitive, emotional, psychosocial, moral and linguistic spheres. This demands a fair understanding of developmental child and adolescent psychology as background knowledge.

Over the decades, sandtray therapy evolved into a creative form of psychodynamic treatment in which children, adolescents and, sometimes, adults can represent their inner world, as well as their personal, family and social circumstances, in a symbolic fashion by working with a multiplicity of toys and objects in a sand-filled tray.

Working therapeutically in this manner might very much enhance the patient's awareness and comprehension of past trauma and, in turn, promote the expression and working through of unresolved feelings and fears, with a view to moving on up.

Although sandtray therapy may look like child's play, it is a highly beneficial and multidimensional form of psychotherapy that can provide emotional release and realisation for adolescents and for some adults too. Those grown-ups who have been traumatised and show poor response to other forms of therapy may respond well to one of the sandtray techniques.

In fact, sandtray therapy may help deeply wounded adults by beginning to facilitate change on a fictitious level, so they might gain the courage and ability to recognise that similar changes could be made in their own life (Sangganjanavanich and Magnuson, 2011).

Severely traumatised children and adolescents, even adults, tend to remain silent for fear of further harm; they may present themselves in highly anxious states and are often unable to verbalise their emotions, when they come to therapy. The reasonably relaxed and flexibly interactive setting of sandtray therapy provides them with the initial arena of safety that they very much need.

In different ways, sandtray therapists act as guides for their patients to fully engage with the world they create in the sand. Patients always remain the focus of the process; the therapist is there to encourage, support and guide them as they depict elements of their inner world in the sand.

Through creative expression, patients may become able to manifest in this type of therapy the problems they would otherwise not be able to vocalise or address in other therapeutic interventions. The patient can add water to the sand and place the miniatures in the sand tray in any order (Linzmayer and Halpenny, 2013).

The design of the sand tray is guided by their imagination and, of course, by their unconscious processes. The result can be seen as a microcosm of their inner world. Indeed, the world within the sand tray is expressed through symbolism and metaphor, although it may not immediately make sense to the person creating it. However, aided by the therapist, patients can start recognising the relationship between what they have created in the sand and their own world.

One of the outstanding strengths of the present book is that it is rooted in a *secure base* of more than one hundred years of child and adolescent mental health, from which it explores and digs deeply into the therapeutic applications of the sandtray technique, whilst integrating the domains of trauma, resilience, parental skills, personal development and neuroscience, within a framework of attachment-based thinking and practice.

The authors emphasise the healing potential of meaningful emotional connections between patients and therapists over the, sometimes, detached exercise of intellectual interpretations.

Trauma is a profoundly distressing and disturbing experience. Inspired by the work of Jorge Barudy and Maryorie Dantagnan, their teachers, José Luis Gonzalo and Rafael Benito often have to deal with a type of cumulative and complex trauma that occurs on a regular or recurrent basis. This is usually described as "developmental trauma", since it can seriously disturb and damage the healthy development of the child, not only in the short term but also in the long-term, if no remedial or therapeutic action is taken (Barudy and Dantagnan, 2005).

Early adversity may include parental mental illness or substance abuse, losing a parent or both, not having enough food, clothing or shelter and various forms of domestic violence, including neglect or abandonment, as well as emotional, physical or sexual abuse or a combination of these (Ezquerro, 2017b).

Ultimately, from the perspective of John Bowlby (the 'father' of attachment theory), trauma is a major rupture or deprivation of protective, caring and loving attachment relationships.

When children are exposed to continuous or persistently overwhelming distress or abuse and the parent or attachment figure is unable to mitigate it, or is even causing it, these traumatic experiences would most likely lead to developmental trauma.

To various degrees, this manifests on the physical, emotional, cognitive, psychosocial, spiritual and brain development of these young people, rendering them vulnerable to major attachment difficulties and mental illness, including psychosis, as well as identity problems, learning disabilities and conduct or personality disorders.

Although severe and recurrent trauma and the absence of secure attachment and love, often harm child development, including brain development, the human psyche and the human brain have much plasticity for recovery and for new growth (Rygaard, 2020).

Yet, the task of becoming resilient cannot be done alone; building resilience entails support and understanding from attachment figures and meaningful relationships with other people. In addition, a sense of safe group attachment in the wider community, when it can be perceived as a secure base, promotes resilience.

In the case of children who have been severely traumatised or abandoned by their parents, John Bowlby decisively believed in the positive developmental influence of adoptive and foster families, sensitive mental health professionals and carers, helpful and inspiring teachers, loyal friends and supportive peer groups.

As a child psychiatrist and adult psychoanalyst, Bowlby also believed in his patients' capacity to develop resilience, to heal and recover from traumatic experiences. In his attachment-based therapeutic approach, he employed a powerful medical analogy:

> "The human psyche, like human bones, is strongly inclined towards self-healing. The psychotherapist's job, like that of the orthopaedic surgeon, is to provide the conditions in which self-healing can best take place."
>
> (Bowlby, 1988: 152)

This is an injection of hope, like the caring and convincing message from José Luis Gonzalo and Rafael Benito in their book. Whether you work with children, adolescents, adults or families, I would encourage you to read it: for instruction, for joy, to become a better, more compassionate and confident person and professional.

London, September 2022

Dr Arturo Ezquerro is a London-based consultant psychiatrist, psychoanalytic psychotherapist and group analyst, who trained with John Bowlby in child and adolescent psychiatry at the Tavistock Clinic (1984–90). He is a senior assessor, teacher and trainer, Institute of Group Analysis; honorary member, International Attachment Network and World Association of International Studies; former head, NHS Medical Psychotherapy Services,

Brent; author of more than 100 publications in five languages, including *Encounters with John Bowlby* (Routledge), *Relatos de apego* (Psimática), *Apego y desarrollo a lo largo de la vida* (Editorial Sentir), *Group Analysis throughout the Life Cycle* (Routledge).

References

Axline, V.M. (1950). Entering the child's world via play experiences. *Progressive Education*, 27, 68–75.

Barudy, J. & Dantagnan, M. (2005). *Los buenos tratos a la infancia: Parentalidad, apego y resiliencia*. Barcelona: Gedisa.

Bowlby, J (1938). The abnormally aggressive child. *Human Relations*, 19, 230–234.

Bowlby, J (1939). Jealous and spiteful children. *Home and School*, 4(5), 83–85.

Bowlby, J (1988). *A Secure Base: Clinical Applications of Attachment Theory*. London: Routledge.

Dale, M.A. & Lyddon, W.J. (2000). Sandplay: A constructivist strategy for assessment and change. *Journal of Constructivist Psychology*, 13(2), 135–154.

Ezquerro, A (2017a). *Encounters with John Bowlby: Tales of Attachment*. London: Routledge.

Ezquerro, A. (2017b). *Relatos de apego: Encuentros con John Bowlby*. Madrid: Psimática.

Friedman, H.S. & Mitchell, R.R. (1994). *Sandplay: Past, Present, and Future*. New York: Routledge.

Ginott, H. (1961). *Group Psychotherapy with Children*. New York: McGraw-Hill.

Linzmayer, C.D. & Halpenny, E.A. (2013). "It was fun": An evaluation of sand tray pictures, an innovative visually expressive method for researching children's experiences with nature. *International Journal of Qualitative Methods*, 12(1), 310–337.

Moreno, J.L. (1946). *Psychodrama*. Vol 1. New York: Beacon House.

Rygaard, N.P. (2020). Improving the mental health of abandoned children: Experiences from a global online intervention. *American Psychologist Journal*, 75(9), 1376–1388.

Sangganjanavanich ,V.F. & Magnuson, S. (2011). Using sand trays and miniature figures to facilitate career decision making. *The Career Development Quarterly*, 59(3), 264–273.

Slavson, S.R. & Schiffer, M. (1975). *Group Psychotherapies for Children*. New York: Free Press.

Chapter 1

The most frequently asked questions about the sandtray technique

Introduction

Since the release of the book *Building bridges. The sandtray technique,* in which we present the most important aspects of this therapeutic approach and to which the unfamiliar reader should refer- (Gonzalo, 2013) the interest in training in the therapeutic use of the sandtray has been growing. I have given countless workshops throughout the Spanish country to make it known among professionals, so that they could incorporate it into their clinical practice and as a technique for advice. I have shared unforgettable seminars and workshops where the emotional resonance, the connection with the scene created in the box and the connection with the participants have transformed the way in which we access our personal knowledge and that of our patients.

The sandtray technique is an experience above all to **feel**—with the professional help of a co-ordinator—and it is a way of delving into the depth of the psyche that transcends the personal unconscious to track and probe the vast, collective unconscious inhabited by archetypes, *"that formless pattern that underlies both instinctive behaviors and primordial images"* (Robertson, 2011). For example, for a young person, the archetype of resilience attracts images and behaviours that can be drawn from their own experience (e.g., their passion for dancing allows them to express their emotional pain for her traumatic life story). Instead, the sandtray can access images and behaviours that tend to be less personal and rooted in the patient's cultural heritage, whether or not they know it personally (e.g., choosing the mythical Russian dancer Rudolf Nureyev when making a sandtray).

Nobody has felt the same after finishing a workshop on the sandtray technique. At the end of the training session, a deep silence and a feeling of inner connection invade the participants, who end up being aware of the need to experience the technique in order to know its very deep therapeutic scope. For this reason, I think that this is a heartfelt book, full of emotions and experiences, human and useful, as it arises from these three years of work in workshops, with colleagues experienced in psychotherapy and who have made invaluable contributions and, of course, from what I have been

DOI: 10.4324/9781003359111-1

learning for 13 years, every day, during the sessions with my patients. No tray is the same as another, although the themes may be similar (because they inhabit the collective unconscious, which is timeless). Working with a patient with the sandtray technique is a deep, unique, original and once in a lifetime experience. It's a form of intense and authentic emotional connection, if it is done in a safe environment and with complete respect for the person who participates with us.

During these years **issues, questions** and **contributions** have arisen that had not been developed in depth in the first book I published in 2013 entitled *Building bridges,* which is an essential manual to learn the basic *ABCs* of the technique and we recommend to the interested reader to complement this one. It is also a request from the professionals who have attended the workshops: to be able to have a manual that guides them on how to integrate the technique into a therapy model.

For this reason, before discussing this integration, it seemed appropriate and necessary to introduce the questions and issues that have been the common denominator of all the workshops that I have given on this fascinating approach. This will allow us to delve deeper into what we have already described in *Building bridges* and include new knowledge learned over the years from other authors and from clinical practice. In addition, it will make it easier for us to understand the epigraphs that we will later expose, related to the integration of the different methodologies of application of the technique within said therapeutic process.

As we already know, the origin of the sandtray technique is analytical. It connects with the thought of psychologist Carl Jung, and we cannot and should not remove the house brand (sandplay). We don't want to and shouldn't dare do it. Later on, we will see different methodologies to apply it in different ways (sandtray) and within a model of comprehensive psychotherapy which seems most suitable for traumatised patients with severe relationship and emotional problems (the psychotherapy model of Barudy and Dantagnan, 2014); however, the aspects of the approach that are genuinely analytical, and that were exposed in *Building bridges*, must be respected. We deal with them in the answers to the most frequently asked questions that professionals pose in their work with the sandtray technique.

Although we are going to answer these questions with recommendations and general guidelines, we must always consider these two fundamental rules: 1) The technique pursues individual knowledge of the patient; objective statistical knowledge is not the focus of this work protocol. Despite being a scientist who pursued objective knowledge, Jung thought that the development of consciousness is always a heroic effort on the part of the individual (Robertson, 2011). Each person is a world of their own that will require a flexible application of the different phases of the technique, always bearing in mind that **not all** patients can work through all the phases[1] because they are not psychologically disposed to do so, especially people who suffer from complex trauma. In order to implement all the phases—should we get to them –, a period of therapeutic work with the patient will be required, respectfully adapting to their rhythm and possibilities. But the technique is not necessarily less useful and beneficial for that; and 2) Any therapeutic intervention with the sandtray technique must always be done by preserving relational harmony, the emotional connection between therapist and patient, and between the created scene and the patient. They must be able to work while regulating their emotions. One of the therapist's missions is to contribute positively to it. If this breaks, we must immediately find a way to repair the emotional connection and show empathy to the client. Any form of pressure or imposition from the therapist in any aspect of the work with the sandtray—however subtle they may be—has consequences for the therapeutic relationship and can generate rejection and negative reactivity towards the technique. This is especially important for people who come to therapy showing relationship problems or disorders. I will expand on this later.

The most frequent questions that have arisen during the training workshops on the sandtray technique

Question 1: How should the sandtray technique be introduced to patients and what instructions should be given?

The sandtray technique requires first and foremost that the patient perceives a sense of an environment that is safe enough to be involved. For this reason, the participants must have at least one person—apart from the therapist— who stays with them in their daily lives and, in addition and if necessary, can collaborate as a co-therapist in the therapy sessions directed by the professional responsible for the intervention. This is important for everyone, but it has proven decisive and key with minors. The minor must have an adult who takes care of them and satisfies their needs, who protects them and grants them a sufficiently secure bond. If people are not protected in their natural context of life, any therapeutic work must be questioned. For this reason, we as professionals have to do what Barudy and Dantagnan (2005) call the demand analysis.

The **demand analysis** entails evaluating whether the main context the minor lives in not only approves but also supports therapeutic work, before deciding to let a professional intervene and start the psychological therapy; especially in the family setting, when there are serious doubts about the parenting skills of the adults responsible for their care (Barudy and Dantagnan, 2010). With parents with severe and chronic parenting incompetence, **family interventions** often deprive children of benefiting from a protection measure that provides them with a foster family or residential context with competent people who support them so that they can build themselves resiliently (Barudy and Dantagnan, 2010). This is important for all minors, but it is especially important for those who are damaged by abuse— they are very likely to develop insecure attachments, and in the most severe cases, disorganised attachments and/or complex trauma. The clinical and professional experience of these authors confirms that it is unfeasible to propose therapy for a minor without the external collaboration of at least one competent adult who supports the minor, meets their needs and works together with the therapist. Because in order to heal from the consequences that abuse has on the psyche (brain and mind) of developing people (such as children and adolescents), and in order to recover from trauma, a whole support network is needed (school, educational, psychotherapeutic, psychiatric...) where the reference of the minor and his sensitive and empathetic care are the cornerstone of the entire intervention. We cannot and should not propose therapeutic work when the minor is alone. As my admired professor and colleague Maryorie Dantagnan—who has vast experience as a psychotherapist of young victims of abuse and different types of trauma—says, performing psychotherapy is like holding a table. At least three legs are needed: the model (competent biological parents, foster parents, educators...), the therapist and the minor. With only two legs (therapist and minor), the table topples over.

Once this *sine qua non* condition is met, the therapist and the patient (older or younger) must establish a **resounding relationship** that encourages thinking in images—the sandtray stimulates this way of thinking: in images, which are represented by the miniatures. Therefore, the qualities of the therapist, such as the ability to tune in (capture the emotion and align with it) and connect (reflect empathetically) with the patient are essential. We will address this crucial aspect later.

There are no set rules about how to introduce the sandtray to patients. In my opinion, and from my experience, a first natural and non-invasive approach to the technique is in the therapy room itself. There are some professionals who prefer to have a separate area of the practice where they place the shelves with the miniatures and the sandtray. However, it is more appropriate for the entire tray set to be in the same therapy room, to make it part of it—like other techniques or materials—and accessible at any time during the session. In addition, if the tray is always with the patient in the same space, within its limits, where all the sessions take place, it will give a sense of security and permanence that benefits patients.

The arrangement of miniatures on shelves is mandatory. Some professionals argue whether they can be kept in bags or baskets, but the truth is that getting rid of the shelf causes the technique to lose all its visual and kinesthetic appeal—many miniatures pose or adopt certain expressions or attitudes, as well as its therapeutic power. The miniatures and items must always be ordered and distributed by categories and the shelves where they sit clean. The miniatures represent archetypes and archetypes are divided into categories, hence their classification in different shelves. In addition, it helps to structure the patient's mind and gives them the peace of mind and security of knowing where the miniatures or items they use to create his scenes are located. Many patients—especially minors who present complex trauma and have suffered abuse, neglect and/or mistreatment—need the therapeutic space to favour physical staying power (Rygaard, 2008). When the patient enters the therapy room and looks at the shelf with all the miniatures in order, a feeling of curiosity, interest and connection with the technique is activated, consciously or unconsciously, thus enhancing the ability to think in images.

We have to make the following exception when placing baskets on the shelf: we often do not have a miniature or specific item that the patient asks for to create their box. In these cases, it's a good idea to have various materials (paper, plasticine, sculpey modelling paste, glue, wool, small balls to make eyes, pieces of cloth…) in baskets, so the patient can create the symbol.

All of this is already a way of implicitly introducing the sandtray technique.

When patient and therapist have decided to work in the session using the sandtray technique, one way to introduce it is to give the patient some brief, direct and simple instructions. Keep in mind that some participants start creating with little or no instruction. This sometimes happens with minors, who are much more spontaneous, in general, than adults. For children and adolescents who begin to make the box by themselves, it is enough to tell them that they can create whatever they want and that the only requirements are not to pour the sand out of the tray and stick to the space in the tray to build.

Other people will need us to approach the shelf with them, take a miniature in our hands, give it to them so they can see and feel it and invite them to touch and play with the sand—to experience the sensory and kinesthetic part that relaxes the *self* of the patient and encourages them to create with fewer defence mechanisms. All this can act as a stimulus for them to start getting involved in the process.

Other patients, on the other hand, are more indecisive and show more defences. It is also possible that they do not understand, or think that they have to do something nice, creative… They are usually patients who tend to judge everything they do (or fear being judged by others) and have a predominantly rational mind. Fear of being wrong—or perfectionism—can constrict your creative flow.

Lowenfeld (1993), one of the inventors of the technique, states that there are three ways of experiencing—and therefore, also of approaching—the sandtray: 1) The one based on the physical and the body; 2) The one based on the intellectual/cognitive; and 3) The one based on the emotions/sensations. When one type of energy is required, it takes over the focus of the mind at the expense of the other modes. The therapist, as Rae (2013) states, must pay attention to these three modes as part of the intersubjective field. Some clues to observe which of these predominates in the patient are:

The **physical mode** becomes more apparent when patients are using the body or moving the sand and objects using few words; somatic expressions are observed by—and experienced together with—the therapist.

The **intellectual mode** can become manifest when the patient uses a significant flow of words and phrases, and verbal language predominates in their expression.

The **emotional mode** can be distinguished when the patient uses shorter sentences, without long grammatical structures, moments of deep silences and an intense emotional resonance with the therapist.

The **balance** and **flexibility** in the activation of these functions is a symptom of balance in people's health. An encounter between patient and therapist working with the sandtray can be rich when both parties access the experience with openness towards the three described modes: intellectual, physical and emotional (Rae, 2013).

For adult patients who approach predominantly in an intellectual way, who struggle to open up to the sensory/emotional and bodily dimensions—it would be desirable for this type of patient to learn to experience these other two dimensions when working with the sandtray—the instructions can be the following (in general, these are appropriate instructions for all patients when we do not know them very well yet):

> "As you can see, on this shelf there are various items that represent symbols that populate the external and internal world of people. You should simply choose the items that appeal to you and place them in the sandtray as you wish and to do whatever you want. Nothing you do can ever be wrong (this instruction is important for this type of patient, and in general for all). What we are looking for is exactly what you represent. The only two rules to keep in mind are: don't throw the sand out of the box (this may be obvious for older people, but maybe not so much for some more impulsive children) and stick to the space of the box. I am your moderator; I'm going to help you with whatever you need. I am available, but it is your box, and you make it. When you're done, let me know. If you don't know which items to choose, let them choose you. Let yourself go; you don't need to think too much. Let yourself flow and let the items and miniatures guide you. This is a different experience from the rest that you have been able to live. You won't be judged or rated."

(This can be useful for underage perfectionists who believe they have to do a nice job, like at school or in high school.)

With children, we adapt the language to their level of maturity. Generally, minors tend to flow and be more spontaneous. Reminding them not to throw the sand out and create the world inside the box is usually enough.

In some workshops (and also in the book *Building bridges*) we added the slogan that it is necessary to **remain silent**. Silence helps the patient to concentrate in their inner self and, at the same time, connect with the technique. Of course, they should not be interrupted by calls or other distractions (mobile phones, etc.) that can break the mind's creative flow. When making the box, we know that the patient's right hemisphere is activated, as well as the contents of their implicit memory. And this must not be interrupted or disturbed by any stimulus. Implicit memory is one of the different types of memories produced by the mind. This will be explained along with the other types, in the chapter: *"Neurobiology of the sandtray technique"*, written by Rafael Benito Moraga, psychiatrist and psychotherapist, teacher of the diploma in child-systemic trauma-therapy.

Anything that alters this peak moment –or any other moment of the session- with stimuli that interfere with the process should be avoided. We insist that silence is important, but not all verbalisations should be prevented in the creation phase. Although some patients do not speak, others do. For this reason, I have chosen not to give them the instruction to remain silent in advance, but to wait and see if they verbalise or not. In the event that they do, I observe what they express with their words. There is a question below that addresses this issue and explains how to proceed; therefore, we refer to it to continue delving into this issue.

For patients who connect with the technique from the body and from the emotion/sensation, the subsequent exploration phase will be very useful to be able to process the entire experience, including the intellectual/cognitive mode, and to balance themselves in this sense. Later, we will address how to also stimulate the body and emotional/sensory level for patients who need treatment in this line. (We will see how the therapist reflects the patient's verbalisations from the figures and items inside the world in the sandtray.)

Some patients will need us to explain to them all about the phases of the technique; additionally, at the end of their representation we stop for a moment to observe the scene. Then we will sit down with them, if they wish, and we will go through what they have done, as if they were inviting us and showing us their house or something very valuable to them. We must show ourselves as respectful, interested, curious and honored to learn about what they can represent on the tray. Finally, we tell them that we will photograph it—with their permission—as it will help us to keep a record of their work with the boxes; later, we can go back to explore it together as many times as necessary and useful for them. We will end up collecting everything and putting it back to its place.

Other people, on the other hand, tend to let themselves go more and connect with their inner self, their body and thought in images. Basic instructions will suffice they can do what they want; there is nothing they can be wrong about; they must not throw the sand out of the box, and they must stick to the space of the box to build what they want.

Some people—in my experience, usually children—will set out to also create outside the sandtray. As already stated in *Building bridges*—we are not going to dwell on this here—we must encourage to do it within the physical limits of the box; this is more than a surface to place the sand, it is a container of experience. It is possible to negotiate with certain minors and circumstances to work outside the sandtray, but only in these specific cases and trying to assess what need the minor wants to express when making this request. The norm should be to build within the physical confines of the sandtray.

In any case, the therapist's ability to inspire trust and safety, including the environment where the session takes place, as we have mentioned above, and responding with empathy to any resistance, doubt, fear, suspicion, questions, are the best way for the patient to overcome these obstacles. We have to make it clear to them that no one will analyse, judge or impose meanings on what they do. The patient is the expert in their box. We must keep in mind that some patients may come from therapeutic experiences with distant professionals and interpreters, where the therapeutic relationship has not been considered, respected or valued.

It is normal for patients to feel fear of being judged or harmed, particularly when they have suffered terrible experiences of abandonment, mistreatment, invalidation of their thoughts; when they have not been seen or felt or suffered physical and/or sexual abuse. For this reason, a good answer to their doubts is usually the one that Rae (2013) gives her patients: "Who's the boss of this world?" As she writes in her book *Sandtray: Playing to heal, recover and grow,* encouraging the patient to enter the world of the sandtray with openness and curiosity is one of the best attitudes to support.

We must avoid telling patients to tell or narrate a story when we give the instructions, as encouraging them to do so stimulates the intellectual/cognitive mode—processing through the left hemisphere—and not the "image thought" more typical of the right hemisphere, which is what we want to prompt in this phase of the world creation (Gómez, 2013). We can explain to them that the technique favours the access to the images of our right hemisphere and that reaching this type of cognitive activity will help us to get to know ourselves better and solve our problems in a deeper way. We will expand more on this in the chapter on the sandtray and its neurobiological correlates, prepared by the psychiatrist and psychotherapist Rafael Benito Moraga.

Question 2: Where should the therapist stand with respect to the sandtray and its building space?

The best place to stand, observe the work and help the patient with their task is one that does not interfere with their movements and actions. The patient stands on one side of the box (not on the narrowest side, but on the longest side that forms the tray rectangle) and the therapist in front of them, without hindering their passage and at an intermediate distance (see Figure 1.1).

However, I usually ask the patient if they are comfortable with that distance. Some patients who have suffered physical and/or emotional abuse and mistreatment feel uneasy about physical proximity, which activates traumatic contents and feelings of insecurity. They cannot explain it; it is not perceptual knowledge, but **neuroceptive** (Porges, 2011). They are invaded by a feeling of insecurity, fear and anxiety that bothers and blocks them, or makes them feel the need to flee or escape. For this reason, with these patients we have to take great care of this aspect: ask, be respectful and, above all, show empathetic receptivity to what they feel, trying to repair and create a safe neuroception. Approaching the sandtray in a state of hyperactivation or hypoactivation is a variable that corrupts the results, impedes the processing of information in the brain and breaks the relational harmony between patient and therapist, the most sacred part of the entire therapy process. On neuroception and other neurobiological issues Rafael Benito Moraga, psychiatrist and psychotherapist, will expand in detail in Chapter 7.

While the patient is creating, we do not adopt his or her perspective of the sandtray: therefore, we do not stand by their side. We place ourselves—as you can see in Figure 1.1—in front of them. Therefore, when taking notes and making a graph on the paper about how they place the miniatures, we must keep in mind that our point of view is different from theirs. When we get to the phase when we observe the created scene and we walk together with the patient to see it from different perspectives, we can look at it from their point of view, i.e., from where they created the scene or whatever they represented.

Question 3: How many miniatures and items are needed? Is it necessary to use sandtrays with water?

When we hold workshops, participants frequently ask how many miniatures we need. Some often comment on how expensive it is to acquire a large number of items and miniatures, in terms of time and money. We must take it easy. We can consider making an initial investment to then progressively, in the long term, provide our patients with a wide variety of symbols to choose from.

When starting to work with the technique, I recommend getting a basic kit that includes diversity—an important aspect: items and miniatures must be displayed on the shelves where you can find variety—making, as we say, an initial financial investment. Some miniatures can be found in stores that sell bags and sets (for example: trees and vegetables; domestic and wild animals; superheroes; from fantasy and movies; rocks and building elements).

You can start working with patients with about 150 miniatures and items. Gradually, and over time, we can continue to make one-off investments—and request them as gifts from our friends and family!—which will increase our collection. Some professionals who have participated in the workshops and I have met later have shared with me the satisfaction of having achieved a fairly complete shelf within a year. From here on, in

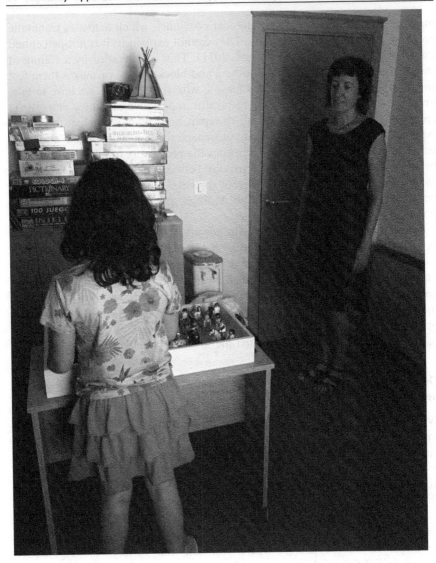

Figure 1.1 The table on which the sandtray rests is normally placed perpendicular to the shelf

our day to day... it is a joy to walk through the cities and, suddenly, find a store where, waiting for us, there's that miniature we want to add to our collection, or one that fascinates us for its originality! And so, little by little, the number of miniatures on our shelf will increase.

It is important not to forget to have symbols that reflect the concerns and needs of our patients, as well as those that represent their culture. The idea is to have as many items, elements and miniatures as possible so that our patients can choose from a wide range.

The therapist miniature shelf also expresses a lot about the therapist's personality. In the initial basic kit, approximately 150 miniatures, which is what I usually carry in a bag to the workshops I give in different cities, we should include these categories: family; animal family; wild animals; domestic animals; humans; professions; trees, plants and vegetables; rocks, bricks and logs; fire; boats and vehicles that move through the sea; land vehicles (cars, trucks, buses, motorcycles...); houses and other buildings; fences; bridges; warriors, soldiers and policemen; good Witch; bad witch; fairy; mythological and terrifying beings; superheroes; firemen; doctor and nurse; kids; babies; some characters from fantasy and fiction (some that are popular at the time); table, chairs, plates and glasses; characters that symbolise good and evil. And lately, we have emphasised the need for pebbles, coloured balls, ribbons, decorative elements, grass, plants, flowers, among other things (see Figure 1.2).

We might not have a miniature or specific item that our patient needs. The possibilities are so endless that this usually happens with some frequency. In that case, we help the patient by letting them represent it on paper or plasticine, if they want to. As we have already mentioned above, the professional must have a small basket of materials visible to the patient to build figures or symbols not represented in the figures arranged on the shelf.

We offer the client the **opportunity to use water**, although it is not a mandatory requirement. By including it, we add new and infinite possibilities because the properties of the sand change (it can be shaped, dug, spread...) and we introduce new sensory and kinesthetic elements that are appropriate and necessary to work with patients who need to stimulate the sensory mode. In this case, you have to have a sandtray with water and another without water, which can be used with a sprinkler.

We can also have several sandtrays at various heights, so that they are within the reach of younger children, or a table that can be raised or lowered to adjust it to the patient's height. I have not treated many preschool children, but the technique is ageless. The experience with this type of child consists of play and is predominantly sensory motor in nature. The little three-year-olds that I've worked with in therapy on occasion are much more comfortable with the sandtray on the floor.

Question 4: Should the tray be made of plastic or wood? Should the sand always natural?

I have worked with a plastic sandtray as a professional for most of the years, trying to adjust as much as possible to the recommended measurements, approximately **70 x 50 x 8 cm**. I think that the recommended height of 8 cm

Figure 1.2 The psychotherapy room that José Luis Gonzalo has in San Sebastián (Gipuzkoa, Spain)

for children is too short, as they tend to go over the edge and throw the sand out. **I usually use a tray that is at least 12 cm high**. The technique can be used using a plastic tray. Recently, I have replaced it with a wooden one because it is warmer and connects us with nature. However, I must say that I do not observe any differences between the use of a plastic tray and a wooden one in terms of therapeutic results, at least not in a blatantly clear way. We can work well with both trays.

The sand should be natural, beach or river. Sand is an element of earth, a symbol that links us to the origin: from it we come, to it we return, as they stated in Ancient Greece. The sand must be fine, pleasant to the touch and clean. Artificial sand generally lacks these qualities and is usually less advisable. However, we can use a different type of sand, it all depends on the effect that we want to cause to the patient, what we want to work with him or her (Homeyer and Lyles, 2021).

Question 5: How long does it take to do a sandtray therapy session? What do we do when a patient takes a long time to build a scene?

There are no rules as to how long it should take. It's obviously not a task that should be timed. Lowenfeld (cited by Urwin & Hood-Williams, 1988) considers the realisation of a sandtray as *"a presentation of an aspect of the internal state of the patient"* Therefore, depending on that internal state, the execution time may vary. For example:

Socrates, an 11-year-old boy whose father died two years ago, agreed to start working on the loss he had suffered. We decided to make a sandtray about the loss of a loved one in general. He certainly felt prepared: he mustered courage and bravery and did it. His self was indirectly present in that sandtray, having activated all the modes (emotional, intellectual and physical) of the experience, especially the emotional one; he connected with sadness and grief, but he also expressed hope for the future. On top of that, when he finished his tray, he said "I'm going to do it again the next day. I'm not happy about it, I'm not focused because I didn't get much sleep and because I had an exam today. I've done it too quickly; I've expressed myself as I always do". It is true that he did it very quickly: he used to spend a large part of the session making his tray. And so it was: by recreating it, he was much more satisfied and discovered aspects of himself and of the whole experience that had not emerged before. As a psychologist-psychotherapist, something like this had never happened to me.

At one end of the spectrum there are patients who take too little time to do the sandtray and at the other end those who take excessively long. In between those ends, then, different amounts of time can be taken. Those who take very little may not have connected with the sensory/emotional mode and with the body. Their way in may be predominantly intellectual. They are usually representations with few items, leaving a lot of free space in

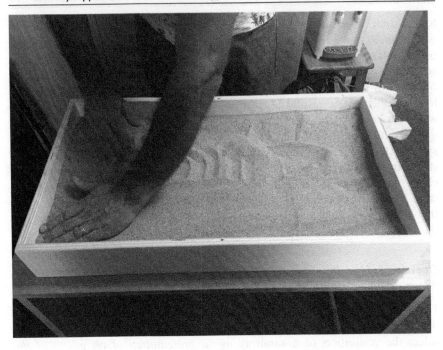

Figure 1.3 One person caressing the sand

the sandtray. They are uncomfortable in the exploration phase, they respond from a rational, linear, literal, verbal mental scheme, showing difficulties to connect and resonate emotionally with the experience of the sandtray, both with the created world and with the therapist. With these patients, we should not ask too many questions that encourage an intellectual approach and prevent the other ways of understanding the experience (sensory and emotional). This is more typical of patients with avoidant and disorganised attachment. The way to work with them is to adapt the technique according to the phase of the therapy. We must begin with an emotional psychoeducation and use the tray to teach them how to connect with the body, formulating questions that delve into this line, that reflect what has been created and that help the patient to experience it little by little, without analysing it from the left hemisphere. We will explain this later, in the section dedicated to sandtray and therapy. We will put up a new clinical vignette of Socrates himself illustrating how we helped him—before he made this tray—to develop emotional skills.

Those who take a long time can remove and put various items and miniatures. They change positions, set and unset part of their scene in the tray once or twice. Some doubt a lot, they are not sure of what they want to do,

Figure 1.4 We can see the world created by Socrates about the loss

sometimes they get overwhelmed, they cannot shape or concretise their internal world in a thought in images. Perhaps they are overwhelmed, excessively anxious with the experience, they cannot structure what they want do. They may be patients, although not always, with an anxious-ambivalent or disorganised attachment type. These patients will also benefit from a specific job adapting the technique according to the therapy block. Structure and intellectual order can help them because they may not have a balance in this regard. Other clients may be perfectionists, afraid of being wrong; their judgments and beliefs about what is right may be activated. They may ask, *"Is this okay?" "Can I use this miniature?" "Is this what you asked?"*, thus reflecting their insecurity.

An example of a world that took a long time to make the sandtray: Ana began by placing several houses with families made up of two fathers and two girls, but then she took them off. Afterwards, she began to build the scene that we see in Figure 1.5 Before making a decision, she changed the position of the store and the house several times. She only placed the stone path made up of small bricks at the end. She thought a lot and was also slow organising and placing the miniatures and items. She often looked at the therapist as if seeking approval. Emphasising that nothing could go wrong was necessary. This seemed to make her feel more encouraged and confident. She was able to end the tray world, although it took almost the entire session, and the joint exploration was brief. We repeated this phase over the following sessions, photographing the tray and taking a video.

Ana was very insecure in her life in general and suffered from symptoms of separation anxiety which are reflected in the following scene. The parents live in the house on the right with their daughters. The girl sleeps, so she can't find out what's going on, the unforeseen events that they won't tell her about. The two younger brothers sleep in a tent, and the two houses are joined by a path made of bricks. "The daughter will be able to go there… but not yet. The parents allow the children to go, but the eldest daughter is scared."

Figure 1.5 The world built by Ana, a nine-year-old girl whose parents requested psychological treatment as she refused to go to school, owing to separation anxiety

This tray was used to discuss how to foster a more secure bond with the parents in order to ensure that Ana achieved secure autonomy, as she manifested features of an anxious-ambivalent attachment. Her parents were too inconsistent in their affective bond with the girl, showing sudden changes and inattention in daily routines which caused anxiety and insecurity in her (for example: parents of other children would look for her after school without giving her any notice).

We can reduce, and even help to overcome these insecurities and the ways they show up when making the tray if we remind patients that nothing can go wrong and that they are the bosses of their tray world. In addition, we must emphasise that thinking is not necessary: being there is more important, flowing like a river, letting yourself get carried away by intuition. Conversely, there will be times when patients require long-term work with the sandtray and with other techniques within a restorative therapy process (such as the one that we will describe later), as they present complex trauma, attachment disorder, dissociative manifestations and associated pathologies and cannot make the sandtray with the three modes of experience with balance and flexibility.

Professionals who use the sandtray must not overwhelm and pressure the patient about time. **We must remember that nothing must break the relational harmony between patient and therapist.** It's important to remember that we are here to support and be patient moderators. What we can do, at a given moment, is to help them by reminding them that there is little time left to complete the task. This must be done in such a way that we are in tune with the client, without disrupting the process and pointing out that we are just trying to encourage them to focus and be able to conclude the representation. If there is no time to explore the created world together afterwards, it can be done another day using the photographs. We have already mentioned that not all patients can do all the phases of the sandtray; for some—especially when the internal world is very chaotic or empty—getting to make a representation with miniatures in the sandtray is a triumph and we must validate and honour this. For these people, giving physical form to what they feel and/or think using miniatures is a great achievement. Such is the case of traumatised patients, whose ability to tune in and regulate emotions is greatly affected as a result of mistreatment, abuse and/or neglect.

Question 6: Is it necessary for the patient and therapist to remain silent during the world-building phase? What to do if the patient speaks?

Silence during the sandtray creation phase, as we have already discussed, is important. The therapist remains silent and concentrates on observing everything that the patient communicates, both with their body and their actions: the miniatures they choose, where they place them, if they make any changes, how they shape their world. Everything is an object of attention for the therapist, who takes notes and records the session on video (there is a question on this subject which we will address later). In addition, the therapist is focused and interested in assisting the patient in their work and their needs. The therapist does not ask any questions while the patient is creating their world in the sandtray.

It is desirable that the participant also remains silent during the sandtray creation phase. However, if the patient speaks, not all verbalisations are of equal value. If what they are saying is not related to what they are doing, e.g., their work with the sandtray, we must kindly remind them that they must focus on the task and not get distracted in those moments with other topics that may cut off their creative flow. We can also give them some feedback to help them focus back on the tray.

If the patient talks about what they are doing, about any aspect of the formation of the tray world, our response depends on whether they describe or explain. The descriptions, to which Rae (2013) refers are a way to support the resonance and the link with the sandtray and their experience with it. However, if the patient focuses on intellectual explanations about the world he is creating, we will encourage them not to do so. Describing is not the same as explaining. Now, a distinction must be made between an *intellectual* explanation to avoid connecting and an explanation that seeks to give meaning to what has been created. The therapist must be cautious of this subtle difference.

Question 7: Can the patient change what was originally placed in the sandtray?

Patients often ask to use certain objects (those off the shelf should not be used), to add water, or to change what was originally formed. That is not a problem. What is more, we can take the opportunity to let them know that they do not need any permission to use the materials or make the adjustments they need in their world. And that our role is to help and assist to facilitate the process, not to direct them in any way. A dialogue in response to what the patient asks serves to clarify and gain security and does not distract them in any way.

Question 8: Is the silent contemplation phase important?

The answer is yes. This phase is very important. In workshops, this moment often tends to happen quickly, and it should not be. We must take all the time that the patient needs. Why? Because, as stated by Gómez (2013), if the phase of elaboration of the world predominantly activates the right hemisphere, the contemplation of the scene in the tray (looking at it with the patient, slowly walking around it) increases awareness and begins to activate the left hemisphere. The corpus callosum—a bundle of fibres that connects both hemispheres of the brain, one of the bridges between hemispheres—begins to transmit information from one hemisphere to the other; what is verbal and what is non-verbal interact and integrate, with the support, the guidance and the help of the therapist. We will expand more on the way the brain functions in this process in the chapter dedicated to neurobiology.

The visualisation of the sandtray brings the patient closer to contemplating it as a whole. This visualisation, moreover, is shocking to many people. Seeing their internal world captured and represented in that transitional space (Winnicott, 2009) through miniatures and items that shape the world increases awareness and connects with the experience from the sensory and emotional modes. For this reason, the patients ask to make changes to the created scene quite frequently. These changes must be allowed, of course.

We should not rush into starting the exploration phase. We must proceed calmly and slowly. When we see that the patient has sufficiently contemplated their world in the sandtray, or when they tell us that they have, we invite them to explore it together. So, we sit down, preferably facing each other, with the sandtray between us.

Most patients often want to share their world and explore it together. In the event that the patient refuses, we will respect their wish. *"They'll have their good reasons,"* as my professor and colleague Maryorie Dantagnan often says. At another time we can try to discuss with the patient the reasons why they do not want to explore the tray together, without pressure and with a friendly attitude. In my experience, if we show empathic receptivity and open up with curiosity and respect to patients' resistance, this will be better resolved than if we confront them and discuss their motivations. In this sense, the authors of psychotherapy from the theory of attachment and intersubjectivity support the need for the therapist to resolve the relationship problems that may arise between the two throughout the therapy with empathy. Affective communication favours psychological healing (Marrone & Diamond, 2001; Ogden & Fisher, 2016).

While we contemplate the world created by the patient -walking around the tray with them, standing quietly and observing with openness, curiosity and genuine interest- we can put ourselves in a place where we can see and carefully feel the world from the patient's perspective.

Question 9: What questions can be asked in the exploration phase?

In the book *Building bridges,* there is a section dedicated to what and how to ask in the joint exploration of the world created by the patient in the sandtray. In this book, we are going to focus on new approaches and ways to co-explore a sandtray.

In Chapters 4, 5 and 6 of this book we will describe in more detail what kind of questions can be formulated depending on whether we are in Block I, II or III of therapy[2]. We will not work with the patient in the same way in one block as in another. As we will see, Block I focuses on emotional connection and regulation; in this block, the questions asked to walk the patient through the process (as opposed to instruct them on it) will influence the way they emotionally reflect what they express about their world in the tray. They will help them to stay in the experience and to connect and regulate the emotions they may feel in the present moment.

In Block II, the questions will focus on reflecting the emotions related to empowerment: being aware of one's power in the face of trauma, emotional problems or conflicts and the resilient areas that the sandtray may contain. Lastly, the questions in Block III will focus on bridging the world of the tray (or a multi-sandtray process) and the real world. We will help the patient to integrate a verbal account, which should not be intellectualised, with their emotions and sensations to favour the sense of coherence of their *self* over time (for example, when a scene from their life story is represented; or traumatic, adverse events from their life). The questions asked in Blocks I and II can possibly be asked in III. However, with patients who are not prepared and require prior emotional connection and regulation work—especially if we deal with people presenting complex trauma—it is advisable not to formulate the questions of Block III until we have adequately worked on the first two blocks.

As far as the joint exploration phase is concerned, here is what we now want to consider:

When we explore the sandtray together with the patient, we should encourage them to do so from within their own world, from within the tray, focusing on **it**. Therefore, we set our eyes on the sandtray and not on the patient's face or eyes, so that they do too.

Asking questions tends to activate logical thinking. For this reason, the therapist is very careful not to shoot a series of questions one after another, with hardly any pauses; imagine being football goalkeepers who are being thrown balls at, one after the other, and not being able to stop them. We raise questions making sure there is silence between the words and delicately drawing the patient's attention to the emotional mode, reflecting what they express, always using the same words and naming the miniatures with the same word they use -letting the therapist put name to the miniature can be a way of directing. We walk the patient through the process, trying to feel and see the patient's mind and the meaning that this tray has for them, avoiding suggesting—much less imposing—our meanings. Otherwise, we may be projecting our emotions and content onto the patient. The supervision of all therapeutic work is necessary and key to being aware of this and being able to avoid it.

When exploring the sandtray, the therapist does not put their hands, body, or other things on the sandtray space.

We try to be interested, formulating the questions without asserting and tentatively, as if they were speculations to verify (this is often quite difficult for therapists because they are not trained for sessions of this type. It requires practice). **The patient is always the one expert in their box!**

We are often going to find that the patient cannot give meaning to one or more elements in the tray, or to miniatures or items. This is normal because not everything can be understood. The world in the sand is revealed little by little. The sandtrays are photographed and subsequently reviewed. In new joint explorations, new perspectives and meanings can be discovered, new questions emerge and the relationship with life and the problems that have led the patient to seek therapeutic help are deepened.

Patient and therapist explore the sandtray together, observing the patient's body and facial expressions. Many times, therapists are more attentive to the story and the words than to the whole experience, including these levels. And this happens because as therapists we are more interested in understanding for ourselves; as professionals, we are often limited by a certain megalomania. Observation and emotional attunement with the patient at a bodily and emotional level is very important because it will allow us to realise if we exceed their window of emotional tolerance (Ogden & Fisher, 2016). In chronically traumatised patients, this tolerance level is very narrow; once they exceed it, they dissociate/disconnect from work (and are no longer in the experience) or become hyperactive (anxiety, anger, fear, intense discomfort overwhelms their ability to handle it).

The co-exploration of the world created in the sandtray is under the control of both participants (patient-therapist). They can become united by an imaginative bond by immersing themselves in the imaginary world of the tray but remain aware of the outer environment.

The author Rae (2013) offers us a list of guiding questions to help in the co-exploration of the tray, illustrated in Table 1.1 They should be suggestions, not instructions.

Once the patient has already told us the name of a miniature, we can say: "We already have a name for this figure." "What do you call this?"

When we use the technique for the first time and we do not know the patient well, or for patients who present a very narrow window of tolerance for emotions, we can refer to Table 1.2. Here are questions that

Table 1.1 Questions that can be asked to help the patient explore the world created in the sandtray (Rae, 2013)

"Tell me about..."	"...the one in the corner"
"Let's take a moment..."	"...to look at the item in the water"
"I wonder about..."	"...the figure that appears to be sitting"
"Let's learn more..."	"...about the man in green who seems to be lying down"
"Let's find out more..."	"...about that castle, house, boat..."
"Tell me about the features..."	"...of this world"
"Please describe to me..."	"...that area you call desert"
"Let's stay a little longer..."	"...to see what we can learn"

Table 1.2 Questions that can be used to help the patient to explore the world created in the first sandtrays or when the margin of the window of tolerance to emotions is very narrow

---

Do you want to tell me about what you have represented here?

What is happening in this world?

What do the miniatures do?

How does (name the figure with the name used by the patient) feel? (This is for patients with enough emotional psychoeducation)

Is there some kind of relationship between the figures?

If there are different areas in the sandtray, we can ask about them, one by one, and find out if there is a relationship between them. If there are bridges or fences, ask about their function.

Does this world need something?

You can ask some more questions about an item, figure or area we need additional information about, e.g.: "Tell me about the man in the gray suit"—use the same words the patient used

If the therapist strongly feels that the patient needs to make a change or introduce something new, they can suggest it. But it must be a suggestion!

---

guarantee a safe distance with respect to what is represented in the sandtray. That way, patients with complex trauma and attachment disorder can access the joint exploration of the technique will be less likely to get overwhelmed or disconnected.

Question 10: When should a sandtray session end? How can a bridge between the world of the sandtray and the real world be created?

Typically, therapy sessions last approximately 60 minutes. There are certain patients that may require more time, so we can foresee 90 minutes, not more, because it can be exhausting and unproductive. **Time therefore imposes a limit.** We must bear in mind that the session includes disassembling the tray, returning everything to its place, checking the sand in the tray in search of possible items (especially the smallest ones) that may have been buried and cleaning the floor from the sand, which is what normally happened with small children.

The therapeutic work with a sandtray—that is, closing the exploration phase and leading the patient to the post-world-creation phase—can end before the session time is up. The patient can go beyond the emotional tolerance window—let's keep in mind that the person, outside this window, cannot process information and the experience with this technique is intellectual, but also sensory and emotional—and begin to communicate with their gestures, body language, uncontrolled crying (liberating, non-overwhelming crying is beneficial), or their own words that they cannot carry on.

Or sometimes, they may get angry or express rage. A pause with silence while being fully present with the patient, showing empathic receptivity, synchronising affectively with them (Schore, 2003) to help to regulate their emotions (restructuring their right hemisphere), are ways of repairing expressions that are probably contents of their implicit memory. But apart from offering help, we must ask if they want to continue or prefer to close the session. *"The most important thing at all times is to safeguard the harmony of the intersubjective relationship"* (Rae, 2013). In the next chapter we will delve into the neurobiological components that come into play when we work with the sandtray and how we can influence them.

Children, as Rae (2013) refers, can show us this break in harmonic resonance in another way: they can ignore our verbalisations; give us a negative look; shake their head denying everything; turn their head and body away from where we are sitting; get out of the sandtray; block their vision of the world in the tray with their hands or their body, etc.

In some cases, we may not tune in and connect well with our patients, and we may not achieve affective synchrony (a dance similar to that of a mother-infant in a secure attachment relationship) with the patient. Or we have pushed the accelerator excessively with too many questions, not respecting the patient's pauses or pace, and this does not favour relational harmony. Sometimes, when a patient has become emotionally overwhelmed (they have gone outside the window of emotional tolerance) and the therapist has contributed to breaking the relational harmony, apologising can be worth a million sandtray sessions. If this harmony has been broken, the therapist must restore it by showing empathic receptivity.

On other occasions, patient and therapist agree that they have sufficiently explored the sandtray world in the session. We can say to them: *"Okay, well, let's wrap this up here, shall we?"*

According to Rae (2013), to conclude a session with the sandtray—if the patient is willing and eager to continue, otherwise this can be done another day—we must help them to leave the world.

To do this, we shift our focus away from the sandtray and begin to focus on the real world, speaking directly to the patient's face rather than looking at the sandtray. In addition, we can do a summary of the session by saying, *"Before we leave this world, let's go over what happened here."* Then both discuss the sequence of events from the beginning of the elaboration of the world to the present. If the patient does not start talking, the therapist can begin by trying to use the words chosen by the patient. We can say, *"How do we summarise what has happened?"*

A very common question in sandtray training is how to bridge the sandtray world with the real world. We saw examples in the book *Building bridges*. Now we will propose other ways of doing it, following Rae (2013), an author and reference in working with this technique.

Table 1.3 Questions that can be asked to bridge the sandtray world with the patient's personal realm (Rae, 2013)

How do you react both externally and internally when these experiences that have emerged in the sandtray occur in your daily life?
How can you realistically apply this to yourself in your daily life?
Is there a way to nurture this form of sandtray awareness in your daily life?
What choices did you make in the past? Do you see yourself taking a different path?
Is there anything revealed to you in the sandtray that is important to your life?
How can you use what you have learned today with the sandtray in the outside world?
Take some time to consider the kinds of experiences that have arisen in your sandtray today. Notice the choices you made and try to acknowledge these experiences showing up in your daily life.

We should only raise this when we are completely sure that sharing it with the patient is going to help them with the problems or issues that have brought them to therapy. We must keep this in mind. Following the Barudy and Dantagnan's model (2014), I usually do it in Block III of therapy, when the patient has worked with the sandtray and with other techniques in another way: emotional psychoeducation (Block I) and empowerment (Block II).

To help the patient bridge the gap between the sandtray and their real life, we can do it in the same session having the tray scene at hand, or if there is no time, in another session with photography or video recording. Otherwise, we can address it after building several sandtrays, in order to help them link the work in the tray with their daily life experience (symptoms, conflicts, relationship problems, personality, etc.).

We first start by exploring the personal realm together to later reach a deeper realm: the archetypal and universal. The questions that can be formulated to explore the personal realm appear in Table 1.3, and those

Table 1.4 Questions that can be asked to bridge the sandtray world with the archetypal and universal realm (Rae, 2013)

Is there anything in this experience that comes to mind, a myth, song, TV show, movie, etc.?
Do you know what other people call (use the word the patient used to refer to a miniature)?
Are you interested in knowing what other people call this specific figure?
Do you know what kind of experience this is in general?
Do you know who in the history of mankind has also had this kind of experience?
What can you tell me about the (name a pattern of experience or category that is in the world of the sandtray, for example: mothers, guardian angels, evil, loss of a valuable object, torture, desert, war) in general?
Do you have any idea who in history could represent this figure?
How could another person be in the universe thinking or feeling like this experience?

that can be asked to investigate the archetypal and universal in Table 1.4. These questions are for children (from ten years old), adolescents and adults who have developed the reflexive function (Fonagy, 2004), i.e., patients who have preserved the integration between hemispheres and also the upper and lower parts, being able to use higher order mental actions (Steele et al., 2008). There are patients who cannot work in this way and will require a therapy that helps them with brain integration. For the most damaged patients in their brain/mind, we will use a progressive block approach, as we will see proposed by the psychotherapy model by Barudy and Dantagnan (2005, 2010, 2014).

The patient-therapist investigation of the archetypal and universal scope of the world in the sandtray makes sense because the tray is populated with these cognitive invariants, as Robertson (2011) calls the archetypes: *invariant* because it is constant in time; *cognitive* because it indicates the mind's process of thinking and perceiving. Moreover, the creation of the worlds in the tray causes the archetypes that populate the collective unconscious to emerge. For Jung (cited by Robertson, 2011) the structure of the psyche (let's imagine a large iceberg) is composed of the conscious (the tip of the iceberg), a very tiny part. Under this conscious (the part of the iceberg that is underwater and cannot be seen) is the personal unconscious; it is a small, but larger part than the conscious. And finally, the rest of the underwater iceberg, the largest part, is made up of the collective unconscious –the archetypes- *that gather our vital experiences around them to form complexes. If we remove the layers of personal experiences forming a complex, we discover the archetype that lies underneath; the process is similar to removing the layers of an onion"* For Robertson (2011), the most beautiful archetype is the ethologist Konrad Lorenz when he was mistaken for its mother by a gosling. *"The gosling imprinted the mother archetype on Lorenz."* A psychologist in sandtray training, whose parents come from different nationalities, told me that two miniatures were *"the parents of all parents"* (by peeling back the layers of her experiences about her own parents, she arrived at the archetype). Here another archetype that transcends personal experience to move to the universal; this is why we can and must work at these two levels, if the patient can benefit from it.

Rae (2013) claims that *"history, art, stories, songs, poems, movies and all forms of human expression can give us courage, clairvoyance about life itself within global humanity, or role models about how others have faced challenges or handled suffering without breaking down and with dignity."* Co-exploration of this field, Rae (2013) states, should only be done *"when the experiences about the sandtray are exceptionally clear"*, that is, the sandtray has been clearly explored completely and several times.

Question 11: In the exploration phase, the patient refers to a miniature present in the sandtray with their own name, identifying himself or herself, or to other miniatures as real, specific people in their life. Can this be allowed?

This is quite common in sandtray training, not only with professionals who have often done personal therapy and have training and experience in their work, but also with patients, although less frequently: upon reaching the joint exploration phase, they start talkign about a figure saying, for example: *"This is me"*.

Theoretically, we should encourage the patients not to talk about themselves, but rather about the figure. Why? By limiting the experience of that miniature to *"me"* or *"someone I know"*, we narrow the field so much that the universal aspect that this figure may have been lost. When speaking, for example, of *"my son"*, we reduce the field to the experience that I have about what I know of *"my son"*. On the other hand, *"the son"* or *"a son"* or *"the boy that is sitting"* extend the range of possibilities and open the experience to the archetypal and universal field. It is more appropriate correct the patient so as to say, *"The son who is in my sandtray"* (in the tray with which the patient is working). This instruction usually works to have patient refer to the miniatures this way (Rae, 2013).

The sandtray requires referring to the internal world and working from within that world. It is not the external reality; it is also not the inner reality. It is halfway between the two, in which we must immerse ourselves by talking about it as if it were real. That is why it is more appropriate and has greater therapeutic power to talk about the figures and the items in the box.

Some people have no training or have never learned to work with a sandtray and speak from the point of view of the figures, the items inside it and their space. For this reason, they often keep talking about themselves. If this happens, the focus on the tray and the link to the experience in the tray is lost.

But what if the patient insists on talking like this, or tends to do it this way despite our attempts to re-orient them? We already know that we must not break the relational harmony under any circumstances; so, I've decided to do the exploration phase in the following way. As Maryorie Dantagnan affirms, if the patient's brain leads them to identify beings and elements from their real life, it is because it is necessary to elaborate and process those experiences in this way. It is true that we must stick to the personal area, without going beyond it, but the patient can have a good sandtray therapy session by limiting themselves to it.

Question 12: If one of the instructions is to never put your hands inside the patient's sandtray, what do we do if a child asks us to play with them inside it?

Another issue that can put relational harmony in check. On the one hand, the norm tells us that we should never put our hands inside the litter box. On the other hand, a child asks us to play with them inside their tray after creating it. And what is more, this is a quite common request. What do we do?

The therapist never asks a child to play with them in the sandtray. If the minor makes this request to the therapist, we must bear in mind that *"once the therapist physically enters the world of sand, the relational dynamics are profoundly transformed. The patient's perception can change the scheme so that the tray is "our world" instead of "my world" (…) When the therapist plays in the sandtray we are within the limits of the creator, which can be violated"*. (Rae, 2013) Furthermore, when we lead the game with a child inside the sandtray, we often lose control of the play. If it is fluid, we cannot follow everything that happens when the world is created and recreated countless times.

If the child plays alone in their world, no permission is needed (except respecting the basic rules of the technique). We can photograph the different sequences of the game to record the final result. But if the child asks to play with the therapist, and in order not to break the relational harmony, we can do it as long as we carry it out with caution and following child-centred play therapy (West, 1995). According to this, we carefully tell the child that we need to know what exactly we have to do. We need the child to instruct us on what items we can touch, pick up and move in a way that is useful to them, based on their way of seeing the world. Specifically, if the scene is a war—something quite common in minors—we must collect all the information we were given by the child about the game and the story and learn about the result that he intends to have in advance. In short, we must allow ourselves to be totally directed by the child and scrupulously submit to what they ask of us. However, as in play therapy, there are limitations, such as when the child gives the professional a victimising role, typical of a traumatic game, e.g., requesting that the therapist in the sandtray play kills them.

This mode of play is only recommended for therapists familiar with and experienced in play therapy (Rae, 2013).

Question 13: Can the sandtrays be photographed and the sessions recorded on video? In the case of minors, can they show their photographs to their parents or caregivers and take them home?

We have already mentioned in the book *Building bridges* that it is necessary to photograph the sandtrays. We have also developed this point in the previous questions. Sandtray photography serves several purposes:

For the patient to have their world. It's theirs. They want to have a memory and recollection of it. Dismantling the sandtray causes feelings of pain and grief to some patients. For this reason, conserving photography is conserving, in some way, the created world.

We ask the patient to photograph it from the point of view that they like. The therapist, in turn, asks for permission to take their own photograph and does so from the point of view from which the patient built the world. Taking high quality pictures with the latest smartphones is now possible in any place and at any time.

The therapist tells the patient that the photograph will also be filed in a folder to have a record of all the ones they take, which will allow them to be able to return to the worlds and work with them again.

Very rarely do patients refuse to take pictures of their world in the sandtray. If this occurs, therapists must be receptive and take an interest in this refusal. By responding with understanding and empathy, we will be able to learn what the underlying motivation is and probably resolve it favourably.

If minors ask to take their own photographs, they are allowed to do so. If they wish to show it to their parents or guardians, we will also allow it, except in cases where we have determined that showing the world to parents or guardians is not positive for the minor. In this case, we will tell them that it will be saved in our folder (or office computer) and that when the time comes (if it comes) it will be shown and explained to the parents or referents. Thus, the child will be given the ability and the opportunity to understand, later on, why the photograph was not shown to the adults responsible for their care. We refer, for example, to minors who are undergoing an assessment process in family intervention for being victims of mistreatment and sexual abuse, where taking what has been built out of the safe context of therapy may not be beneficial for the minor.

It is necessary to record the sessions on video. Permission must be requested beforehand; for this reason, in Spain, the patient—or the parents or guardians of the minor—are asked to sign an **informed consent** using the terms provided in Organic Law 15/1999, dated 13 December, on the Protection of Personal Data[3]. The informed consent is prepared by the therapist, given to the patient—or the parents or guardians of the minor—to read and to sign. The video allows us to observe aspects of the entire process that we may have overlooked, as it is impossible to notice everything during the session. Also, there are times in the sandtray session when we cannot take notes because we have to be with the patient. Recording on video makes it easier for us to focus on this task. Finally, we can watch the recording with the patient and work on the tray again and continue to explore it in the following sessions.

Question 14: How and when to take notes? What aspects must we observe and record in a session with the sandtray?

In addition to recording the sessions on video, we recommend that taking notes of the sandtray session.

When taking notes, the main rule is not to disturb the patient's work with the sandtray, making them feel uncomfortable and distracting them from their world-building task. If the patient asks why we are taking notes, we tell them that we want to remember how they made the tray and the most important aspects of the session, so that we can help them to work therapeutically with the tray later.

Notes should be taken from the beginning of the session and until the patient has created the world in the sandtray, that is, until the creation phase. After that, we have to do the joint exploration of the sandtray with the patient, so taking note and working with them at the same time would prevent us from being fully present in the experience and creating the connection between patient-therapist-sandtray. At this time, the session should be recorded. If we want to write down some point or aspect that seems relevant to us, we have to anticipate it and allocate a few minutes—when the patient has already left—before the next session.

As for what is important to record, we have to look at everything: Does the patient first touch or move the sand and then choose the items and miniatures? Is the patient's attention focused first on the shelves where the miniatures are? Do they keep the topography of the sandtray as it is to place the miniatures, or do they shape and re-shape the sand as they shape the world? We can see which zones and items are left as they were which are moved and changed. We look at what the patient chooses and how they do it. Does the patient choose the items and the miniatures one by one or in groups? When some items are taken to the tray, are some used and other not? We pay attention to "accidents": what collapses, is destroyed, found or formed by chance. How does the patient respond to and deal with this? We examine how, where and when items and figures are placed in the arena and any changes made afterwards (Rae, 2013).

In addition, we observe the emotional and behavioural responses of the patient throughout the process. We record how this creation affects us, so that we are aware of our emotions and attitudes. Let's not forget that minors and adults who have suffered abuse and neglect and/or have emotional problems or disorders often create violent, cruel, sadistic, terrifying, deeply hopeless, sad scenarios; we must also pay attention to how they use trees and plants, symbols of life and energy, and how they use protective, resilient, spiritual symbols. Do I feel sad, scared, overwhelmed, angry? Am I attracted to the qualities of what I see or, on the contrary, does it push me away? Am I disconnected, asleep, distracted? Finally, we have to observe the patient's body: facial expressions, sounds, crying, body states while creating the world, etc. As therapists, self-monitoring is the key to perceiving these states and responding to the patient in a way that we can help (Rae, 2013).

In order to make notes effectively, we usually give the students attending our courses a record sheet of a session with the sandtray. However, it is so extensive and wordy that therapists often find it very difficult to complete it in its entirety within the given time. To facilitate this task, I have created a summary record sheet with the essential information that I believe is necessary to write down. You will find it at the end of this chapter.

Question 15: Can we work therapeutically with one or each sandtray or is it necessary for the patient to build several sandtrays?

There are no established rules regarding this aspect. Everything is possible. Our decision will depend on our patient's personality and how the technique can be adapted to them; on the nature of their problem, their disorders or symptoms; and on the extent they are able to mentalise[4].

There are patients who can do all the phases (preparation, creation and post-creation) with a single sandtray, showing a high level of involvement and immersing themselves in the experience from the three modes (intellectual, emotional and sensory). We can even bring them closer to the archetypal and universal. Others, on the other hand, owing to different reasons, are not able to work on all the phases: making several trays and assisting them with a progressive approach, including co-explorations based on the questions collected in Table 1.1 and in Table 1.2, is more beneficial to them. After making several sandtrays, for example, we can get a better, deeper understanding and connection with the personal aspects of their life, the problems that they bring to therapy and/or the symptoms shown.

Especially with patients who present complex trauma and attachment disorder, it is necessary to make a treatment program in which the sandtray technique is integrated and worked with according to the three-block therapy model of Barudy and Dantagnan (2014).

Question 16: When taking the sandtray scene apart, should the patient do it alone, the therapist alone once the patient has left, or both at the same time?

There are three options:

After photographing the scene and ending the session with the patient, the therapist picks up the sandtray by themselves and returns everything to its place. By doing this we miss the patient's reaction, which in my experience does not favour the transition to the real world.

The patient returns everything by themselves, without the help of the therapist, who simply stays by their side and observe how they do it. Some children may have a hard time picking things up without help, but this is a valid option.

Therapist and patient collect everything together, which is my preferred option and the most successful. The patient is the one who puts their hands inside the sandtray (in the meantime, we can notice which miniatures or items are being removed first and from which area of the tray); they can give us the objects so that we return them to their place on the shelves, or they can do this by themselves. This allows us to observe the reactions at the end and share the experience of concluding and closing the session with the sandtray. This way, we can help the patient to definitively enter the realm of reality.

Question 17: Is it possible to work with the sandtray with a directive methodology?

It should be clarified that by using the term "directive" I refer to working with the technique to achieve the goals that the therapist and the patient have agreed to be the object of treatment with psychotherapy. For example, the patient's goal is to *"better understand my emotions and reactions"*, that is what the sandtray work will focus on. What the patient does from here on is not directed at all. The elaborations are made according to what the patient discovers—with the help of the therapist as a supervisor—in the joint exploration phase.

When the patient says they are stuck on a problem, does not know how to explain it, they feel overwhelmed, confused, struggling inside, that is an ideal moment to invite them to go to the sandtray area and connect with it, let themselves go and build what they want.

Conversely, by "non-directive" I mean that the sandtrays will not refer directly to a particular issue or difficulty. There will be therapeutic goals to achieve, of course, but in a more implicit and indirect way.

Both methodologies—which will be explained in detail later on—are equally based on the basic rules to favour joint exploration, the conclusion of a session, photographing and collecting the sandtray.

Although the non-directive methodology is the most conventional, there are authors who opt for the directive mode as a valid approach (Gómez, 2013). *"Those who have used other sandtray models find that they work the same"* (Day & Day, 2012).

The directive approach is probably not the preferred choice when starting with the technique, and not with all patients; it is true that some get stuck in the creative process. But it does turn out to be a useful and valid method for many patients. Personally, I have worked in this way with many, especially with teenagers and adults, and with children who were willing and prepared for it, with excellent results. I usually start with the non-directive approach to gradually approach the agreed goals in therapy in a more directive and explicit way. It is a very helpful strategy when treating and exploring complex traumas like sexual abuse, mistreatment, abandonment, painful losses (death of a parent from an accident, suicide or murder), traumatic situations like war, poverty, violence, hunger, mental and/or physical illnesses, bullying, workplace harassment, etc. With other patients, however, the strategy may be different.

For this reason, in short, the most convenient thing to do is to combine both methodologies, adapting them to the profile of each patient according to what best suits them. Some patients need to feel that the therapist is a safe, strong figure to find the courage to represent certain topics in the sandtray, however hard and painful it may be. Others, on the other hand—less affected by psychological damage—are more emotionally stable, better able to mentalise and self-regulate and show less insecure attachment profiles helping them to process the experience better and to be in better conditions to co-explore the tray of sand, thus needing less strength, confidence, security, courage, pressure from their therapist. In addition, there are ways to propose the elaboration of the sandtrays with a directive approach. It must be done with kindness, curiosity, tact and... as if it were a challenge! When I want to do this with children, I usually say something along the lines of: "*Would you dare to make a sandtray about anger?*" Some find this stimulating and motivating.

Question 18: Is the sandtray only used individually or can it be applied with groups and families?

According to Pearson and Wilson (2001), the sandtray can be used with families and groups. For them, an advantage of working with a systemic approach, inviting a family or group of people to participate together in a session, is that the focus of intervention is transferred from a single person, usually believed to be the one with a problem (e.g., a minor), to an entire group or system. Families work together in the sandtray space and can gain valuable insights into their dynamics. A group work with the sandtray can be an opportunity for authentic expression and listening to the other. You can read more about this in the book of Homeyer and Lyles (2021)

The shared experience of working in the sand improves communication among family members. Lack of communication can be one of the main reasons why minors end up acting out previously inhibited emotions. Group sandtray therapy, the authors say, can enhance a family member's resistance to change, healing or growth.

The therapist must be careful that the group work with the sandtray does not turn into an opportunity to exercise dominance over a specific individual. It is better for the professional to work first in individual sessions before moving on to group work.

Limits and rules must be set beforehand. All the group members must be equally committed to working on the objectives of the session and complying with the rules. If they have already had the sandtray experience individually, it will be easier for them to make decisions and agree on the rules. If the group is new and does not know the sandtray, then the therapist should set the rules. Clients need to know that the session's work object is going to be addressed into the world or what is created in the sand.

Pearson and Wilson (2001) collect the rules that are usually set when working with the sandtray in a family or in a group:

What are they going to build or do in the sandtray?

How is the space of the sandtray divided?

Who sets the symbols (items or miniatures)?

Is permission needed to make changes to the created scene?

Should the intervention shifts be taken into account? Working in this way, it is important that **everyone expresses their feelings** about the sand scene after they have created and observed it.

Afterwards, the therapist helps all the members to co-explore the scene or world in the sand. They can be invited to describe it, and also reflects emotions and takes advantage of silence to help connect all members with the world in the sand and with each other. The questions that can be asked are those that we collect in the tables. In order to get to explore the personal and family environment—i.e. linking what happens in the sand world with the family in real life—the members must be able to benefit from this kind of work. Therefore, the therapist will dedicate a significant amount of time to analysing and understanding the origins of the problem and family dynamics and relationships. In-depth knowledge and training in systemic orientation are required to make good use of this tool.

This way of working with the sandtray technique is not the subject of this book. The reader interested in delving into it can refer to the books: *Sandplay and symbol work*, by Pearson and Wilson (2001) and *Sandplay therapy with children and families*, by Carey (1998).

Question 19: Is it important to take into account the patient's level of mentalisation when making a sandtray?

We have already mentioned this skill is and that it must be taken into account. We are now going to focus on this topic in detail, referring to what we have previously written (Gonzalo, Cáseda & Benito, 2021).

Since the moment when the patient stands by the shelf, observes the miniatures arranged on it and a tray with sand close by, the technique is already exerting a mentalising influence, arising a lot of curiosity. *"What is this for?"*—many beginners ask. And curiosity is one of the main ingredients of mentalisation-based therapy (Bateman & Fonagy, 2018). When we explain what it consists of and they notice that there is nothing they should know, nothing they can be wrong about, no judgment, just a process where reassurance and empathy rule, defences go down and curiosity and intrigue increase. The presence of imagination and the playful aspect of the sandtray favour the involvement of the patient and their openness to learn what they have built in the world in the sand. Some people may be concerned and anxious about not controlling what may come out. Their emotions are validated, they are shown empathic receptivity, and they are encouraged to create because they truly are the experts at what they do. Even those who refuse to work with the technique receive empathy and validation, as it is probably not their working method, and they will have their reasons for it. Understanding this makes the patient feel understood.

The therapist is not the one who knows: they are the one who, together with the patient, will try to infer the mental state of the miniatures and understand the meanings of the different symbols, if required. They will try to make sense of the nonsense. The collaborative stand of the two, where there is not a person who knows (therapist) and another who does not (patient) makes it a supportive process where the two team up to learn about what happens in the representation in the sand. In fact, what is staged in the sand is the patient's own psyche—which is why the therapist never reaches into the world—turned into physical form that can be touched and moved within a space/time dimension. In order to mentalise a psychic content, there is nothing like externalising it and turning it into a thing (a miniature) that can be named and that can have meanings and/or generate emotions in the patient (both the miniatures individually and in relation to other miniatures and elements). Many people find a sense of distance, security and emotional regulation by projecting themselves onto third elements, as long as the therapist knows how to support them and turn the sandtray experience into a process where mentalisation is not lost. Hence the extreme importance of tuning in with the patient and recovering relational harmony with the patient, if it is lost at any time.

When the patient has finished creating the world in the sand, silently observing it and contemplating it as a production of one's own mind, quietly looking at it from different perspectives (as it does look different) and validating the experience and the invitation to speak or not about themselves, this makes the patient understand that they and the therapist are sharing and having a representation of the patient's mind in a space that is halfway between fantasy and reality.

It can be a world whose representation is close to the reality the patient is aware of, or an imaginary world. At a given moment, if the world in the sand is linked with the patient's real world, bridges can be built, and we can learn how to bring that learning to the life of the patient. Like when a movie, play or painting (a performance) teaches us about ourselves. That is why autistic spectrum patients cannot normally work with the sandtray: if they do not have a sufficiently developed theory of mind, they can't differentiate between fiction and reality.

Patients who are in simulation mode (Bateman & Fonagy, 2018) can create scenes reflecting their perception of real life that is far diffrent to their reality; for example, a victim of incest represents idyllic, loving families, respectful of the limits of the body, just the opposite of what they have lived. They are not ready to leave the simulation yet, because it is too painful to verbalise it (Müller, 2020). They need to create those worlds to defend themselves from a confusing anguish, that is, knowing that they have been abused by their father. Patients who are in equivalence mode may struggle to distinguish themselves; emotions invade them in such a way that they either cannot access representations, or these are unstable and changing. It is possible that they first need to learn to stay, feel and let themselves go with what they experience, with the therapist acting, validating and regulating their experience, because feeling their own raw emotions—e.g., rage—can cause them to want to finish the tray and even attack and assault it. Finally, patients in teleological mode will not see the sense of the technique and will probably not want to participate in the process, because its function does not lead to a practical goal or end.

The peculiarity of the sandtray makes it an ideal technique for working with people's mental states in the exploration phase. If the basic premise of mentalisation-based therapy (Bateman & Fonagy, 2018) is to access someone's inner world with curiosity, interest and motivation to learn, the sandtray takes this to its fullest. When the therapist takes a mentalising stand, what they do is asking and not knowing. This happens whenever we help the patient in the co-exploration of what is represented in the arena: we do not know anything, we are going to try to understand together; and the therapist is a facilitator in this process of knowing the mind, never an expert.

There is another factor that makes the sandtray technique an outstanding mentalising process: attributing mental states to the miniatures in a projective way, so that the mentalisation projected on the miniatures and the different items that make up the world is worked on the sand. It is an attempt to reflect and understand oneself, but through or a nonverbal and verbal symbolic representation; it is not just the words are taken into account, but also and especially the image and the sensations to which we learn to give meaning with words. This gives the patient enough distance and security so as not to inhibit the mentalising processes: on the contrary, perceiving it as non-threatening enhances them. The fact that no mistakes can be made, and the patient is the expert in their world in the arena makes this procedure impressive to work and infer the mental states of the different protagonists that populate the scene in the sandtray and offer the opportunity to reflect on them. For patients in general, if the link is secure, and respect and empathic receptivity is shown, they are encouraged to learn about what has been staged. There are also times when not understanding the presence or function of certain miniatures fuels mentalising desire.

As we'll see throughout the book, the kinds of questions used to explore the world in the sandtray are completely mentalising. In fact, they all meet the key principle proposed by the creators of mentalisation-based therapy (Bateman & Fonagy, 2018), which is to stop, rewind and reflect. If we review these questions, we will see that they encourage to inquire about the mental states of the characters and items. For example:

How does the farmer feel?

What does the farmer think?

What does the farmer need?

What would happen if...?

I wonder if the farmer might feel sad...

What do you think the farmer might think...?

The same as when the sandtray is explored from mindfulness, silence and with questions with the purpose of understanding what comes to the patient's mind by looking at the world in the sand, a character, a certain area or a specific item.

And sometimes, when everyone in the sand is a metaphor, it becomes a meaningful mental representation that allows the patient to understand their mind and what is happening to them.

And finally, the archetypes (Robertson, 2011) that populate the collective unconscious of people (or the link between the world in the sand with the universal sphere) emerging in the sandtrays of patients can be considered as the highest expression of a complex and superior mentalising process, as we need to resort to the symbols that a community uses in order to understand ourselves. When we resort to universal symbols such as Mother, Father, a Path, Light, Darkness, Peace, Order, and so on, we approach an understanding of our sense of self that allows us a deeply reflective and revealing mentalising process. For example, the homosexually oriented dancer who had to confront his father to claim his freedom to be both a homosexual and a dancer, feels understood when he discovers a universal character that gives him meaning Nureyev, an icon in the world of classical ballet.

Question 20: What are the limitations and precautions in the use of the sandtray technique?

Another frequently asked question in sandtray workshops. Although in the book *Building bridges,* we already mentioned some counter-productive effects of the technique, here we collect more considerations on the matter.

Although many patients are willing to manage their problems and show a positive attitude towards healing self-reflection, there are some **situations** in which **the sandtray technique is not encouraged** (or should be applied with caution and at the client's pace). These are (Pearson & Wilson, 2001):

The patient showing strong resistance to working with the sandtray.

The crisis level requires immediate action and there are environmental demands that the client needs to address. Work with the sandtray can be postponed until later in psychotherapy. We must assess whether the context protects and keeps things under control.

The level of emotionality and energy is high, and the patient needs a more direct intervention to work on emotional liberation.

The client has a history of emotional instability and has been hospitalised, owing to acute mental disorders.

The client has an addiction and does not have an appropriate environment to deal with their problem.

The patient is unable to differentiate between the symbolic world and reality. The distinctions between internal and external world are not clear. Such is the case of people on the autism spectrum who have not developed a theory of mind (Baron-Cohen, 2012). There are specific protocols for working with these patients, you can see Homeyer and Lyles (2021).

A wide variety of objects and items and the sense of freedom (to create whatever the patient wants) seem too threatening, as can happen to some hyperactive patients or patients with a highly disorganised attachment. In this case, it is convenient to limit the work to a smaller number of items and miniatures.

Children with tactile hypersensitivity or sensory integration problems, who are hyperexcited by contact with the sand.

Here, we will develop a comprehensive model—neurosequential (Perry et al., 2013, 2017)—of psychotherapy where we introduce the sandtray technique. Each therapist must make their decision: it is necessary to know why, for what and how we explain the problems of the child, adolescent or adult who puts themselves in our hands so that we can help them heal, sometimes from very painful, complex wounds. A technique devoid of a paradigmatic foundation is *technique for technique's sake*, running the risk of getting lost and not knowing what we are doing or where we are going. **The psychotherapy model we are committed to** (Barudy and Dantagnan, 2014) **allows us to apply the sandtray technique with patients on a scientific basis.**

The technique in its most authentic form, which we have exposed in this section and is now concluded (how to introduce the technique, the creation phase, the questions to ask in the co-exploration phase, etc.) is compatible with work through intervention blocks according to the neurosequential psychotherapeutic model of Barudy and Dantagnan (2014). As I apply the technique with this model, I will illustrate the experience that I have been acquiring in the various workshops and especially within the APEGA Network[5].

Later, we will further explain the two methodologies of work with the sandtray in therapy: the non-directive and the directive. In the following sections, we will apply them within the model of Barudy and Dantagnan (2014).

Finally, in Chapter 7, as a climax, the expert in this scientific field, my dear and admired psychiatrist Rafael Benito Moraga **will offer a fantastic, fascinating journey through the neurobiological structures and processes intervening when using the sandtray technique psychotherapeutic context.** This is for us to be aware of the changes and positive modifications occurring in the patients' brain when using the technique. Recent research shows that we can modify the affected neural networks and repair them through psychotherapeutic interventions, which is why our vision advocates escaping from classical dualism: conceiving the human being as an entity whose brain and mind are indivisible.

Summary sheet of a session with the sandtray[6]

NAME: _____	PHOTO N°: _____
DATE: _____	SESSION N°: _____
THERAPIST: _____	

I. Creator Approach (Underline those that apply)

Easy/Difficult start   Able/Unable to get involved in the process

Decided/Doubtful   Managed internally/Externally

Space use:
All/Part of it   With/Without purpose Verbal/Non-verbal

With/Without care

Water use: Yes/No

Place items and then change: Yes/No   No. of scenes:

II. Objective description (Underline those that apply)

A. Tray organisation:

Empty/Overfull   Open-close/Fenced   In action/Static

One idea/Several   Ideas Rigid/Realistic   Organised/Chaotic

Without people/With people

B. Miniatures and items used and placement order

C. Significant verbalisations (story) during co-exploration of the scene (attention to verbal expressions and affective tone, body expression as well as metaphors and themes to highlight in their speech)

III. Assessment (General Impressions/Clinical Analysis)

A. What are the predominant themes in the sandtray? (Observations and comments on the topic(s) in the sandtray: how you organise and express them. Points of conflict and strengths)

B. Suggestions and recommendations for diagnosis and treatment

C. Other relevant comments

Notes

1 To learn about the application phases of the sandtray technique, the reader can refer to the book *Building bridges. The sandtray technique* (2013) published by Desclée de Brouwer. We do not intend to repeat them here and cause a déjà vu to the experienced reader.

2 The reader can go to section two of this book to learn about the three-block Psychotherapy Model by Barudy and Dantagnan (2014).

3 NB: this is a Spanish law. Readers should consult the prevailing legislation in place in their own country about this issue.

4 Wikipedia: (Mentalisation) the ability to understand the mental state –of oneself or others– that underlies overt behaviour. Mentalisation can be seen as a form of imaginative mental activity that lets us perceive and interpret human behaviour in terms of intentional mental states (e.g., needs, desires, feelings, beliefs, goals, purposes, and reasons). It is sometimes described as "understanding misunderstanding." In a way, mentalisation means being able to "read in behaviour what is going on in the minds of others." At the same time, it is possible to reflexively understand one's own experience and one's own actions. The concept of mentalisation is supported by research on the *Theory of Mind*; it was coined by Peter Fonagy and Mary Target (Fonagy, Gergely, Jurist and Target, 2005).

5 The APEGA Network is made up of all the professionals who have graduated from the Barudy and Dantagnan Postgraduate Course in Systemic-Child Traumatherapy in its different promotions in Catalonia, the Basque Country, Madrid and Chile since 2004.

6 Adapted from SORKARI S.L. Center of Attention to the Integral Development of the Person. Sopela (Bizkaia, Spain).

References

Barudy, J. & Dantagnan, M. (2005). *Los buenos tratos a la infancia. Parentalidad, apego y resiliencia*. Barcelona: Gedisa.

Barudy, J. & Dantagnan, M. (2010). *Los desafíos invisibles de ser madre o padre. Manual de evaluación de las competencias y la resiliencia parental*. Barcelona: Gedisa.

Barudy, J. & Dantagnan, M. (2014). *La trauma-terapia sistémica aplicada a los niños, niñas y adolescentes afectados por traumas. Un modelo basado en los buenos tratos y la promoción de la resiliencia*. Powerpoint presentado en el marco del Diplomado en trauma terapia infantil sistémica. Bilbao: Documento no publicado.

Bateman, A. & Fonagy, P. (2018). *Tratamiento basado en la mentalización para trastornos de personalidad. Una guía práctica*. 2nd ed. Bilbao: Desclée de Brouwer.

Carey, L. (1998). *Sandplay therapy with children and families*. Maryland: Jason Aronson Book.

Day, C. & Day, R. (2012). *Creative therapy in the sand. Using sandtray with clients*. United Kingdom: Book Creative Therapy.

Fonagy, P. (2004). *Teoría del apego y psicoanálisis*. Barcelona: Espax.

Fonagy, P., Gergely, G., Jurist, E. & Target, M. (2005). *Affect Regulation, mentalization, and the development of self*. New York: Other Press.

Gómez, A.M. (2013). *EMDR and adjunct approaches with children. Complex trauma, attachment and dissociation*. New York: Springer Publishing Company.

Gonzalo, J.L. (2013). *Construyendo puentes. La técnica de la caja de arena (sandtray).* Bilbao: Desclée de Brouwer.

Gonzalo, J.L., Cáseda, T. & Benito, N. (2021). *Traumaterapeutas en la caja de arena.* Barcelona: Sentir Editorial.

Homeyer, L.E. & Lyles, M.N. (2021). *Advanced sandtray therapy: Digging deeper into clinical practice.* Routledge.

Lowenfeld, M. (1993). *Understanding children's sandplay: Lowenfeld's world technique.* Cambridge, UK: Margaret Lowenfeld Trust.

Marrone, M. & Diamond, N. (2001). *La teoría del apego. Un enfoque actual.* Barcelona: Psimática.

Müller, R. (2020). *El trauma y la lucha por abrirse. De la evitación a la recuperación y el crecimiento.* Bilbao: Desclée de Brouwer.

Ogden, P. & Fisher, J. (2016). *Psicoterapia sensoriomotriz. Intervenciones para el trauma y el apego.* Bilbao: Desclée de Brouwer.

Pearson, M. & Wilson, H. (2001). *Sandplay & symbol work.* Melbourne: Australian Council for Educational Research.

Perry, B., Brandt, K., Seligman, S. & Tronick, E. (2013). *Infant and early childhood mental health: core concepts and clinical practice.* United Kingdom: American Psychiatric Publishing.

Perry, B. & Szalavitz, M. (2017). *El chico al que criaron como perro y otras historias del cuaderno de un psiquiatra infantil.* Madrid: Capitán Swing Libros.

Porges, S.W. (2011). *The polyvagal theory: neurophysiological foundations of emotions, attachment, communication and self-regulation.* New York: W.W. Norton & Company.

Rae, R. (2013). *Sandtray: Playing to heal, recover and grow.* Plymouth, UK: Jason Aronson.

Robertson, R. (2011). *Introducción a la Psicología Junguiana. Una guía para principiantes.* Barcelona: Obelisco.

Rygaard, P.N. (2008). *El niño abandonado.* Barcelona: Gedisa Editorial.

Schore, A. (2003). *Affect Dysregulation and disorders of the self.* London: W.W. Norton & Company.

Steele, K., Nijenhuis, E. & Van der Hart, O. (2008). *El yo atormentado: la disociación estructural y el tratamiento de la traumatización crónica.* Bilbao: Desclée de Brouwer.

West, J. (1995). *Terapia de juego centrada en el niño.* México: Manual Moderno.

Chapter 2

Comprehensive psychotherapy model where the sandtray technique is applied: Barudy and Dantagnan's Three Block Systemic Traumatherapy

The psychotherapy model of intervention in childhood psychotrauma we apply to evaluate and to work with the sandtray technique is based on Barudy and Dantagnan's findings on Good Treatment of Children; neurodevelopmental consequences of mistreatment, abuse and neglect; recognition of the victims' psychological suffering; minors' ecosystemic vision and evaluation of parental competencies and parental resilience (Barudy & Dantagnan, 2005; 2010; 2012; 2014). It is also based on attachment theory (Bowlby, 1983; 1985; 1989; 1993; Ainsworth et al., 1978; Main et al., 1986; 1990. Liotti, 2006; Fonagy, 2004; Ogden and Fisher, 2016) and its association with interpersonal neurobiology (Siegel, 2007). The findings of trauma psychology (Porges, 2011; Steele et al., 2008); psychology of development; the notion of permanence and the stages of self-organisation (Rygaard, 2008); and finally, encouraging child resilience (Barudy and Dantagnan, 2005; Cyrulnik, 2003). Therefore, **it is an integrating paradigm whose main domains are attachment, trauma, development and resilience.**

Barudy and Dantagnan's psychotherapy model is used with children and teenagers but given its neurosequential (Perry et al., 2013) conception and application and its epistemological foundations, it can be adapted to adult patients.

The therapists of the APEGA Network[1] have obtained significant clinical practice working in psychotherapy with children and teenagers who were victims of mistreatment, abandonment, neglect and sexual abuse. They were able to confirm how the model enhances their resilience by treating, among many other aspects, two elements that favoured the process: **the bond and the meaning** (Cyrulnik, 2003) or reconstruction of their life story (or "resilient reintegration", as it is named by our friends Puig and Rubio, 2011).

Barudy and Dantagnan's psychotherapy model has the following purposes: Provide the minor with a therapeutic experience that allows them to repair the psychological damage caused by mistreatment, abandonment and/or sexual abuse (therapeutic attachment, a concept promoted by Siegel, 2007). Provide some techniques and a treatment methodology adapted to child suffering. Strengthen the resilience of minors by adding external resources that help internal resources emerge.

DOI: 10.4324/9781003359111-2

Evaluation phase

The psychotherapy model begins with a comprehensive **evaluation of the minor who is doing psychotherapy. This evaluation includes the four main domains that it subsequently affects, namely: attachment, trauma, development and resilience.** The said evaluation is a planned proposal for action, taking into account all the factors and different areas of the damage caused by ill-treatment.

The comprehensive evaluation includes the child, the parents or guardians of the minor and the context. The minor's difficulties, functioning, development, symptoms, attachment profile and the presence or absence of psycho-trauma are thoroughly evaluated.

Parental skills that need to be modified, revised and/or reinforced are evaluated in parents. And in the context, the factors that hinder, amplify or maintain a certain functioning in the minor and prevent their development are assessed.

As the aim of this model is to support and reinforce resilience, it also includes evaluating the child's resources—skills, talents, cognitive abilities, qualities, adaptive traits—as well as the parents' (attachment style, empathy, internal resources to modify models of interaction with their children, extended family and social network) and the context—sensitive and affectionate teachers, with calm authority; health professionals willing to work in a network; extracurricular spaces and other sources of resilience. As we see, an ecosystem approach is fundamental.

Comprehensive assessment sets realistic goals that reinforce and promote resilience.

A Comprehensive Assessment Guideline is used as a tool to collect all the relevant information on the minor and their context in order to plan treatment. It also includes a tree for decision-making, to determine whether psychotherapy can be applied to the minor at the time, based on the combination of certain variables. We have already discussed this before, so we will not expand on it. We again recall the importance of always analyzing any demand for psychotherapeutic treatment.

The **therapeutic relationship** deserves a special mention as it is the fundamental axis on which the entire intervention revolves (including the evaluation phase). If the psychological damage caused by abuse of minors is mainly manifested in interpersonal relationships, it is from and through these that it can be repaired. Experiencing a warm, reliable and safe therapeutic relationship can create new internal working models and generate new interpretations and expectations about the other, their sensitivity and empathy in the minor. Working with minors, therapists associated with the APEGA Network live by the principle collected by the author Holmes (2009) from the first session: *"Good therapists do with their patients what competent parents do with their children".* It is the affective aspect and the quality of the therapeutic relationship that allows us to give meaning and, therefore, resolve the traumatic contents of our experiences.

Psychotherapeutic treatment phase: Three-block Model

Once the comprehensive evaluation is done, the psychotherapeutic intervention phase begins. The intervention Model in Childhood Psychotrauma by Barudy and Dantagnan (2005; 2010; 2014) is made up of three blocks on a good basis; that is, working in parallel with the parents or guardians of the child or teenagers and focusing on promoting attachment, connection and consistent response is essential. The three blocks follow an internal logic based on a neurosequential order, according to a principle proposed by Perry (2013).

According to Bruce Perry (2013; 2017), neural systems organise and become functional sequentially. The key to healthy development is getting the right experiences at the right times. The brain develops from the back to the front, from the posterior and lower zones to the superior and upper zones. It follows an order based on **neurosequences**, in such a way that the environment begins stimulating and connecting the neurons that are in the reptilian brain (the brain stem).

Therefore, children who have experienced trauma present a complex clinical picture, with very unequal functioning in the different areas of development, so the treatment approach must be specific to each situation. The goal is to have a picture of the archaeology of each brain. Barudy and Dantagnan's Comprehensive Assessment Guideline aims to obtain this picture and design a tailored treatment for each child according to the affected areas and to which neurosequence each child is located in, from which they need to be stimulated.

They need repetitive and patterned experiences appropriate to their developmental needs. These needs will reflect the age at which they lost important stimuli or experienced trauma, not their current age. Therefore, one of the main principles of trauma therapy is repetition. Using different techniques affecting different aspects of development, throughout the three blocks of traumatherapy, the child is repeatedly stimulated, through the patience and perseverance of the adult-guardian who believes in the child and supports them in their recovery. This way, what can be learned in each sequence is integrated.

Once the altered brain areas have been identified, therapy should be aimed at stimulating their development and in the order in which they occur naturally (neurosequential), regardless of the age of the minor.

The first neurosequence is the reptilian brain (brain stem, cerebellum and hypothalamus). At this stage, physical contact and establishment of brain rhythm is key. It is the phase of rhythms, rocking, feeding routines, sleeping and playing, soothing the baby with a rocking motion and soft words. The second neurosequence to develop is the limbic system (amygdala, hippocampus, hypothalamus, accumbens and cingulate). In this phase, self-regulation, play, learning of rules and limits, communication and socialisation processes, empathy, etc. are worked on. The third neurosequence includes the development of the frontal cortex, when the thinking brain is born and intelligence and mentalising abilities appear.

All of this work must be done in a context where healthy role models are available: *"The healthier relationships a child has, the more likely they are to recover from trauma and grow up healthy. Relationships are the agents of change, and the most powerful therapy is human love."* (Perry & Szalavitz, 2017)

Barudy and Dantagnan's Traumatherapy follows this principle of neuro-sequential order and each of its three blocks, as we will see below, works on the three neurosequences. For the application of the sandtray, when we work with children, it is very important to know in which neurosequence the child is located so that we focus on a different block. It will be box of Block I (to work the first and second neurosequences), where what we want to achieve is that the therapist approaches the technique while in tune with the experience and within the margins of emotional tolerance, that is, working on emotional regulation; or Block II, where we focus on addressing emotional regulation, attachment, play, neuroaffective communication, the development of psychological and problem-solving resources...; or Block III, where we highlight reflection, because the child can use the ability to mentalise and intelligence.

Table 2.1 Barudy and Dantagnan's Three Block Psychotherapy Model

Neurosequential order principle

Block 1	Block 2	Block 3
Tuning and self-regulation	*Empowerment*	*Resilient reintegration*
Context – routine	Executive function	Specific traumatic contents
Internal motivation	Alternative strategies	Historical narrative
Acute symptomatology	Internal working model	Projection of the future
Self-observation	Identity – self-esteem	Making options
Modulation	Dissociation	Closure
Expression		
verbalisation		

Depth level

Attachment—Emotional Attuning—Consistent Response

Life context

Block I: Tuning and self-regulation

As Siegel (2007) suggests, building a bond is necessary to establish interaction sequences to emotionally tune in with the minor: the left hemisphere of the adult aligns with the left hemisphere of the child or teenager, and the right hemisphere with the right. Once tuned in, the adult emotionally resonates with the minor, making them feel that they feel them. These tuned and resonant communicative interactions favour the child/teenager's ability to self-regulate their internal states.

The therapists of the APEGA Network, aware that young victims of abuse trauma have deficits in this area, focus on working on the following aspects in the first block (in order to be able to help the minor to resiliently integrate the trauma, it is necessary for the patient to tune in with the therapist, with their internal states, as well as develop self-regulatory skills. This block, however, is usually revised in later phases of therapy):

Stabilise routines in the minor.

Strengthen the elements of the context that allow positive bonding, self-control and regulation.

Treat the minor's acute symptoms with the appropriate techniques and, even, with pharmacological treatment if necessary (upon consulting a psychiatrist).

Help the minor develop self-observation skills so that they learn about their internal states and their triggers in different situations.

Provide psychoeducation about the effects of trauma on the brain.

Develop skills of expression and proper modulation of emotions.

Various techniques expressly designed to work with these contents are used in this block. Among these, the sandtray technique can be a very useful tool for the minor to develop the ability to observe, to learn about their internal states, as well as to identify, express and modulate emotions. At the same time, the sandtray enhances the secure bond between patient and therapist.

For example, Loreto is a ten-year-old adopted girl who has lived in a poorly managed orphanage for two years. Her ability to express herself verbally was very limited as a result of abandonment trauma. I felt that Loreto had spent so much time suffering by herself, in her cradle, deprived of the vital nourishment coming from tuned and affective communication with an attachment figure, which is what generates a secure internal model and prepares and designs the brain/mind for emotion regulation. Loreto barely verbalised anything other than functional everyday aspects. Everything related to internal states was practically not mentalised. When I asked her how she was feeling or thinking, she would get stuck and stay silent. This is how she lived for a long time. She had a survival response installed, probably consisting of

Figure 2.1 Loreto's sandtray world let her to know and express her emotions.

disconnecting from herself. I decided that the sandtray could be a good tool to use in this Block I of the therapy. As a matter of fact, we slowly worked on the knowledge and expression of emotions as exemplified in the caption (See Figure 2.1).

Block II: Empowerment

One of the terrible consequences of chronic trauma is usually the feeling of vulnerability, helplessness and a feeling of permanent threat. For this

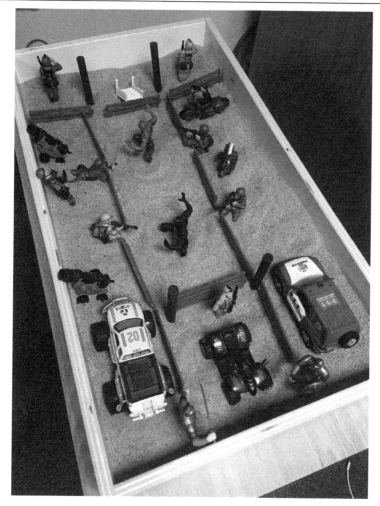

Figure 2.2 The good and the evil in Javier's world on the sand

reason, trauma expert authors speak of **returning to the victim the power they once lost.**

Specifically:

That the minor becomes the protagonist of his own therapy process, in such a way that the therapeutic work is co-directed.

Stimulating the executive functions that may be weakened as a result of trauma, in order to help the minor to respond—and not react—and to make a process of problem solving and planning and sequencing their actions conscious, teaching them to monitor their own cognitive, emotional and behavioural processes.

Learn alternative strategies to trauma-derived mental actions (lower-order mental actions) (Steele et al., 2008).

Make minors aware of their own internal work model and work with its contents trying to modify these representations.

Identity and self-esteem treatment.

Various techniques specifically designed to work with these contents are also used in this block.

The sandtray technique can be used in this block to stimulate executive functions, address the internal working model and learn alternative strategies to mental actions resulting from trauma. Javier, 12 years old, created this scene (see Figure 2.2) where *Black Spiderman* and *Red Spiderman* represent *good* and *evil*—as we can see, he accesses the archetypal arena of the sandtray experience. *Black Spiderman* makes decisions on a whim, he doesn't care how others feel, he's selfish and can do a lot of damage. *Red Spiderman*, for his part, pursues the good, thinks of others and their feelings and makes decisions more carefully. Depending on who prevails in this fight, the soldiers will help or destroy the created world. From here, we were able to work on alternative strategies and anticipate the consequences of the actions of each of the characters. Javier was going through a delicate moment: his personality showed loving, positive and constructive aspects, but he could also be cruel, negative and destructive, particularly with people he had an intimate bond with at times.

Block III: Resilient Reintegration

This is the most delicate and deepening block of treatment, in which the minor requires the most support from the therapist—and from the network—in order to find enough courage and bravery to do the work.

Specifically:

Development of a historical narrative with the minor.

Treatment of specific traumatic contents.

Future projection.

Options and consequences.

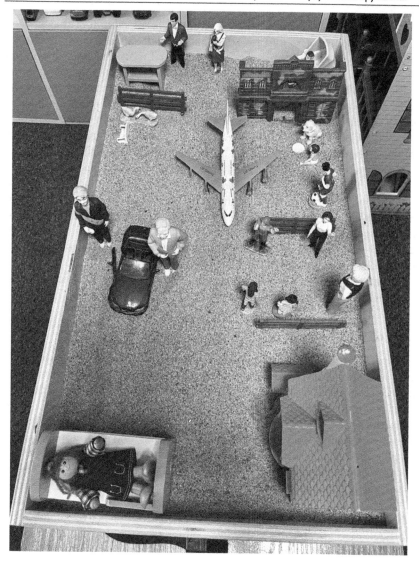

Figure 2.3 The day in which Ismael met his adoptive parents represented on the sandtray

Closure of sessions. This is planned of time and is specifically worked on, since farewell and separation activate manifestations of insecure attachment and traumatic responses.

Various techniques expressly designed to work with these contents are also used in this block.

As for the **sandtray**, it turns out it is a powerful therapeutic tool that favours the ability of the minor to **narrate safely and without so much pain**, processing the experience (from the three modes: intellectual, corporal and emotional) with moderately high levels of anxiety, specific traumatic content and the elaboration of life stories. Ismael, 11 years old, was able to recreate the day he met his adoptive parents for the first time, based on how he felt it, on how he was told about it and also on how he imagined it (see Figure 2.3). There is a fence to the right that separates the town where he currently lives (present) from the orphanage (past) in Russia, his home country. The parents (the adult figures with white hair) and the plane represent the arrival and access to the place where he was living, lying in bed with a mate. The child could pivot and focus on how he felt in that moment, in the "here and now", thinking about that moment in the past; and when he got too overwhelmed, he could concentrate on the safety of the present—here and now too—on his current family and how he was taken care of, and connect with positive emotions. The therapist helped him with all of this.

The therapist must intervene properly so that the minor becomes progressively more involved in the methodology.

Levels of involvement of the psychotherapist

The first level of involvement takes place in the first block. The therapist who works with traumatised minors directs therapy work, takes a proactive, dynamic, managerial role, keeping the minor under control. This is because the minor struggles to get involved and commit to therapy. They are not great at mentalising, their attention span is short, and they get tired easily. At the beginning, they may present more acute symptoms and less motivation for therapy. Complex trauma and disorganised attachment, with a tendency to dissociative states may affect the process. Blocks I and II take much longer and it is usually difficult to get to the third. In the specific case of the sandtray applied to trauma therapy, we try to be empathetic and compassionate and slowly show the technique to the patient. We prioritise above all the therapeutic relationship and neuroaffective communication, and later, when the patient develops confidence and security, give way to verbal communication.

At the second level of involvement, the therapist co-directs therapy work, their participation is rather semi-directive. Therapy is carried out in a balanced way between the participation of the therapist and the minor, which makes the objectives easier to achieve. There is more involvement than in the first level. Initially, symptoms may not be as acute and motivation for therapy may have been achieved earlier. Disorganised attachment may be less severe, or the protective environment has transformed the child's attachment into organised avoidant/anxious. Or it is possible that the attachment was initially organised, although insecure. They may present a higher level of mentalising ability. Blocks I and II take less execution time and the therapist can go deeper. Neuroaffective communication and empathetic support continue to be crucial, but cerebral integration is greater, and the patient can access the verbal story of the sandtray more easily. Thanks to these patients' abilities and body connection, Block III can be done and reached earlier, going moderately deep into it.

In the third level of involvement, the therapist guides or facilitates therapy work. There is a higher level of depth and involvement in the therapeutic process in the minor. As they are equipped with a greater capacity for mentalisation, the patients play a proactive role in therapy, taking ownership of the process. Therefore, therapists like to suggest themed trays for each of the three blocks. Gaining therapeutic attachment made it possible to develop a more secure attachment (Siegel, 2007), acute symptoms that generate discomfort are absent, and there is a stronger emotional regulation: all of this favour the possibility to reach this level, using different psychological resources. Vertical and horizontal brain integration capacity (Siegel, 2007) is achieved, using with the patient can regulate the intensity of their emotions and use words to create a story that gives coherence and meaning to what is represented in the sand. The patient may not present a disorganised attachment to begin with, nor a tendency to present dissociated states, and the impact of the complex trauma on his psyche was milder. They can explore to a great extent in the three blocks, with the therapist as a reliable figure providing safety, regulating and facilitating the work; the patient is the protagonist of the process, and the therapist has a less directive and proactive role.

The therapist has a more directive approach at the beginning in terms of directing therapy work, agreeing on goals, encouraging the patient and having a proactive role, offering safety and transmitting to the patient a neuroception of security and control in the therapy space. However, work with the techniques in general and with the sandtray in particular do not have to be directive. The approach used to build a therapeutic relationship should not be confused with the approach used to work with a specific technique. Working with the sandtray technique, we will opt for the non-directive approach as a general rule unless we think that working with a directive is more appropriate and beneficial for a specific patient. We must not be strict about following the rules, and at the same time be consistent with what each person may need.

Using the three blocks, parallel work with the context of the minor and with the parents or guardians is essential. They support the process, share the objectives of each block, adequately support, regulate and keep the minor under control, participate in resilient integration work, etc. Sessions are planned with the parents or guardians alone to achieve their collaboration, involve them in the therapeutic work and train them in specific psychoeducational skills and techniques (emotional modulation, control, limits, establishment of routines…).

The three blocks are not static: they are dynamic, e.g., the abilities of the first can be used in those of the third. The idea of the block instead of the phase aims to convey precisely that concept of interrelation and communication between contents.

For example, a certain patient can work with a high level of involvement in the therapy and a high level of depth in the therapeutic content, so they can go through the first two blocks faster and become capable of doing a block three with a good level of penetration. On the other hand, if a patient is at the first level, their emotional regulation is much more compromised, their level of mentalisation is low and they lack psychological resources in general, so the therapist must be more proactive at the beginning; they will struggle to delve deeper into the contents, taking longer to carry out Blocks I and II.

Results

After over 20 years of work, the results of the experience with the minors participating in the Child Psychotrauma Intervention Model (Psychotherapy Centers of the APEGA Network of Barcelona, Madrid, San Sebastián, in Spain; and Viña del Mar, in Chile) are generally positive.

We evaluated both the quality of the results, i.e., the improvement expressed by the minor and also verified by parents, guardians and teachers who reported emotional and behavioural changes, and the quantity, through the indicators and questionnaires included in the comprehensive evaluation.

In general, 90 per cent of the participants presented positive changes. These are seen in:

The creation of new mental models of attachment in relation to the other. It improves self-confidence as well as confidence in the adult world.

A greater ability to modulate and regulate emotions.

The reduction in the frequency of appearance of mental actions derived from the trauma (aggressiveness, impulsiveness, hyper or hypo emotional activation…) Minors have a lower score in the trauma indicators.

The disappearance or reduction of the symptoms initially shown.

A more cohesive and integrated sense of self.

A more adequate and positive self-image and self-esteem.

A more defined and less vague identity.

The emergence of resilient resources and more positive interpersonal relationships.

Conclusion

The therapeutic model in childhood psychotrauma allows the therapist to intervene in the domains that are affected as a result of abuse. It has been shown to be useful and effective in repairing psychological damage and promoting resilience. **It is a comprehensive and systematised treatment model, adapted to respectfully deal with the suffering of minors.**

The sandtray technique has emerged as one of the most important techniques and contributes positively to these results. Now, it is necessary to work from an integral model of psychotherapy, which gives meaning to the intervention-and not with loose techniques and devoid of the epistemological foundation that every model provides. A technique, by itself, cannot respond to all the therapeutic needs of a patient, especially when they present complex problems. We use a comprehensive intervention model and program such as that of Barudy and Dantagnan, adapted to each case, multi-component and using various techniques and methodologies, such as the useful and valuable sandtray. It is necessary to be trained in its use, but, as we have been discussing, we cannot exclusively work with it (or with any other technique): in the case of minors, it is also essential to include the parents or guardians of the minor and intervene in the context that surrounds them.

Before concluding this section, we would like to emphasise that the Barudy and Dantagnan Model of Traumatherapy requires training, practice and supervision. It is a model that includes an extensive evaluation and intervention program that requires expert articulation of all the components that make it up.

Next, we will focus on the methodologies to apply the sandtray technique in therapy, within this model of psychotherapy by Barudy and Dantagnan (2014).

Note

1   The APEGA Network is made up of all the professionals who have graduated from the Barudy and Dantagnan Postgraduate Course in Systemic-Child Traumatherapy in its different promotions in Catalonia, the Basque Country, Madrid and Chile since 2004.

References

Ainsworth, M., Blehar, M., Waters, E. & Wall, S. (1978). *Patterns of Attachment*. Hillsdale, NJ: Erlbaum.

Barudy, J. & Dantagnan, M. (2005). *Los buenos tratos a la infancia. Parentalidad, apego y resiliencia*. Barcelona: Gedisa.

Barudy, J. & Dantagnan, M. (2010). *Los desafíos invisibles de ser madre o padre. Manual de evaluación de las competencias y la resiliencia parental*. Barcelona: Gedisa.

Barudy, J. & Dantagnan, M. (2012). *La fiesta mágica y realista de la resiliencia infantil: Manual y técnicas terapéuticas para apoyar y promover la resiliencia de los niños, niñas y adolescentes.* Barcelona: Gedisa.

Barudy, J. & Dantagnan, M. (2014). *La trauma-terapia sistémica aplicada a los niños, niñas y adolescentes afectados por traumas. Un modelo basado en los buenos tratos y la promoción de la resiliencia.* Powerpoint presentado en el marco del Diplomado en trauma terapia infantil sistémica. Bilbao: Documento no publicado.

Bowlby, J. (1985). *El apego. El apego y la pérdida* 1. Barcelona: Paidós Ibérica.

Bowlby, J. (1993). *La separación. El apego y la pérdida* 2. Barcelona: Paidós Ibérica.

Bowlby, J. (1983). *La pérdida. El apego y la pérdida* 3. Barcelona: Paidós Ibérica.

Bowlby, J. (1989). *Una base segura: aplicaciones clínicas de la teoría del apego.* Barcelona: Paidos Ibérica.

Cyrulnik, B. (2003). *El murmullo de los fantasmas.* Barcelona: Gedisa.

Fonagy, P. (2004). *Teoría del apego y psicoanálisis.* Barcelona: Editorial Espaxs.

Holmes, J. (2009). *Teoría del apego y psicoterapia. En busca de la base segura.* Bilbao: Desclée de Brouwer.

Liotti, G. (2006). A model of dissociation based on attachment theory and research. *Journal of Trauma & Dissociation,* 7(4), 55–73.

Main, M. & Solomon, J. (1986). Discovery of an insecure disoriented attachment pattern: procedures, findings and implications for the classification of behavior. In T. Brazelton & M. Youngman, *Affective Development in Infancy.* Norwood, NJ: Ablex.

Main, M. (1990). Cross-cultural studies of attachment organization: Recent studies changing methodologies and the concept of conditional strategies. *Human Development,* 33, 48–61.

Ogden, P. & Fisher, J. (2016). *Psicoterapia sensoriomotriz. Intervenciones para el trauma y el apego.* Bilbao: Desclée de Brouwer.

Perry, B., Brandt, K., Seligman, S. & Tronick, E. (2013). *Infant and early childhood mental health: core concepts and clinical practice.* United Kingdom: American Psychiatric Publishing.

Perry, B. & Szalavitz, M. (2017). *El chico al que criaron como perro y otras historias del cuaderno de un psiquiatra infantil.* Madrid: Capitán Swing Libros.

Porges, S.W. (2011). *The polyvagal theory: neurophysiological foundations of emotions, attachment, communication and self-regulation.* New York: W.W. Norton & Company.

Puig, G. & Rubio, J.L. (2011). *Manual de resiliencia aplicada.* Barcelona: Gedisa.

Rygaard, P.N. (2008). *El niño abandonado.* Barcelona: Gedisa Editorial.

Siegel, D. J. (2007). *La mente en desarrollo. Cómo interactúan las relaciones y el cerebro para modelar nuestro ser.* Bilbao: Desclée de Brouwer.

Steele, K., Nijenhuis, E. & Van der Hart, O. (2008). *El yo atormentado: la disociación estructural y el tratamiento de la traumatización crónica.* Bilbao: Desclée de Brouwer.

Chapter 3

Sandtray and Traumatherapy

The importance of affective communication over interpretation

In the previous section I have highlighted how important the secure therapeutic bond between patient and therapist is, as well as the need to build it throughout therapy. In this section I would like to emphasise the enormous importance of this therapeutic link, and the tuning and resonance of the communication (Siegel, 2007) in the use of the sandtray technique.

Why this emphasis? Because in the workshops that we give on the sandtray technique, most professionals impatiently focus too much on understanding what the patient wants to say, on unravelling the meaning of what they say. For this reason, in my workshops we communicate to all the participants that the most important thing is **affective synchrony** (Schore, 2003) with the patient, the experience of bonding with them and with the scene created and, as we mentioned in preceding paragraphs, first and foremost maintain relational harmony with the person who is with us. Therefore, we want to give this theme a prominent place and space: because **affective communication prevails over interpretation.**

We do not mean that the patient should not be walked through the discovery of the meanings of the symbols that they have used in the sand world and the relationship that these have with their real life and the problems that brought them to counselling. But therapists must introduce this and communicate it at a time and in such a way that they are sure that it will be useful and beneficial to the patients. And, as we have been discussing throughout the work, always trying to preserve relational harmony.

The interpretative aspect of psychotherapy turns the patient into a passive subject and object of analysis. In our model, we discard this intervention scheme. The trays are never analysed, nor is the patient. They are helped to co-explore the created scenes and build bridges with their real life. Any attitude in the professional that leads to imposing interpretations that are meaningless to the patient, insisting that the patient is holding back, trying to resolve this resistance by alluding to interpretations is far away, and in our view counterproductive, from a model that prioritises emotional connection with the patient, empathic receptivity and the construction of a solid

DOI: 10.4324/9781003359111-3

therapeutic bond, which is what really contributes to psychic and emotional cure and healing. A student in a workshop told us: *"What I liked the most is how well supported and cared for I felt at all times"*.

The sandtray is an experience in which the three modes -intellectual, sensory and emotional- must be combined in harmony. Working exclusively with interpretation and on a language devoid of connection with the other ways of experiencing the sandtray does not make it easier to process the experience. And when it is processed, the two hemispheres (left and right) collaborate closely. This is when the integration of traumatic contents, self-states or memories of emotions and sensations occurs.

Thus, we must prioritise affective communication over understanding and meanings. In such a context, these will be progressively revealed to the patient when they are ready, as trust and confidence in the therapist will be the secure basis to start exploring. Patients -like babies when they enter the autonomy phase- discover and are open to the new and ready for interpretations if they have a secure bond with their therapist. As the non-threatening nature of the environment allows them to turn off their attachment system, they feel calm, free, confident and, above all, safe to be able to explore and discover the world around them. Babies also know that their attachment figure is available in case they need protection from any threat. They activate the exploration system and develop better than children whose attachment is insecure at all levels, because they experience more and therefore learn more. In the same way, patients whose bond with the therapist is secure -because they trust that problems, conflicts, obstacles can be overcome together- will dare to build the sand world and want to co-explore it in depth and interpret its meanings related to their life and problems. We have discussed this in the previous section about the psychotherapy model of Barudy and Dantagnan: the relationship between patient-therapist must become a **therapeutic attachment** for the patient (Siegel, 2007).

Therapeutic attachment is especially important when we treat and work with patients with complex trauma and attachment disorder in early childhood (they are likely to present personality disorders in adulthood). These patients have a **neuroception** of insecurity, fear and suspicion towards people. Alan Schore (2003) tells us the following: the stage that goes from 0 to 18 months of age is crucial because it is when the child develops what Porges (2011) calls **safe neuroception**[1]. What safe neuroception favours is that the social connection system (seated in the ventral vagus nerve that goes from the spine to the cortex), which regulates us emotionally at an internal and interpersonal level, predominates and conforms adequately at the expense of other branches of the nervous system (sympathetic / dorsal vagal) created for defence, which are the ones that work and are easily stimulated and hyperactivated when the neuroception created is one of threat or alert. That is why many of these children—or adults—are ready to react, because they have absorbed sensations, emotions and environments charged with hostility, threat, risk, unpredictability. Therefore, with all patients -especially with those suffering from complex trauma and attachment disorder- it is vital that therapy with the sandtray technique becomes a tool that favours the expression and re-elaboration of contents and psychic experiences that are too painful to address exclusively with words, and that provides a harmonious relational experience, in affective synchrony, that can contribute to safe neuroception. Many children work with the sandtray and play with it feeling that neuroception of security.

The conflicts that arise in therapy, the misunderstandings, what therapist and patient feel, the different expectations, **everything that concerns and affects the therapeutic relationship and breaks the connection must be given a fundamental value** (Ogden and Fisher, 2016). Because talking about what has happened between therapist and patient and offering reparation (attending to what the patient feels, accepting and respecting them, validating their emotional world—which could be tremendously invalidated—showing curiosity, openness and empathic receptivity) is how we really contribute to the patient's healing. We have all been confirmed and disconfirmed by our parents or caregivers in some respects. Even those with "imperfect but still secure attachment" (Bromberg, 2011; Ogden and Fisher, 2016) may also have unmet needs and emotional problems. What happens is that patients with complex trauma and attachment disorder suffered severe and continuous disconfirmations that concern the most important basic securities. Such was the case with Julian.

Empathy helps overcome resistance with the sandtray

Let's examine a practical case: Julián is a 17-year-old adolescent who lives in residential care. He must leave the reception centre in a year and begin the stage of emancipation, with all the uncertainties and real fears that this entails. In addition, he lacks any type of family support; he is a victim of severe sexual abuse and mistreatment in childhood, he has no contact with either his father, the main abuser, or his mother. Both have severe and chronic parental incompetence, making it healthy for him to stay out of any relationship with his parents (siblings are not willing to help him) so in the short-medium term he must find a job, a place and some people to live with. He is going through a very delicate stage. His symptoms are theft, outbursts of anger and aggressiveness against property when frustrated, substance abuse and sadness and deep crying when he connects with his life and circumstances. He did not want to go to psychological treatment under any circumstances, but the judge, after an assault on private property, imposed it on him as a condition to avoid admission to a centre for legal action.

Julián attends few sessions, and when he does, he barely collaborates. He is clearly uncomfortable, tense and nervous, especially if the questions are personal. When we discuss theft, referring to his behaviour (what happens before stealing, during, after...) he collaborates more because he wants to work to solve this problem that has brought legal consequences.

One day, finding it difficult to put into words what he wanted to express to me, I invited him to do it with the sandtray. That day Julian was late. Suddenly, he began shouting as if he was surprised and irritated at the same time, and said unpleasantly:

JULIÁN: "You think I got up today and came here to make a f**king sandtray?! Who do you think you are?! You think I'm an idiot, you too like the others, telling me what's good for me and what isn't? No, no, no...!

THERAPIST: (*Breathing first, I didn't expect this reaction*) I'm sorry. I don't think I've picked the right time to ask you this. I'm sure you've got your good reasons to get angry and not wanting to do the sandtray. Sometimes people don't know how to pick the right time to do things.

JULIÁN: It's just that you think you know everything, just because you've studied, you've got your titles! And no, no... life is something else and you have no f**king idea!

THERAPIST: I didn't mean to give the impression that I know everything, not in the slightest. I'm sorry. I was just trying to show you a way of expressing yourself that I thought might make you feel more comfortable than talking.

JULIÁN: I'm not having a good day today! (*With a frown on his face*)

THERAPIST: When we're having a bad day, we don't want to feel overwhelmed, we want people to let us know that they feel how overwhelmed we are. If I had known, that's what I would have done. I didn't know you had a bad day today. If I had known, I wouldn't have shown you the sandtray. But when I ask you how you are, you usually tell me that you're fine, and I didn't ask you to tell me more because I noticed that you don't like it – please correct me if I'm wrong. I usually go on to work on the topic of theft, which is what we have agreed. I thought the sandtray might work for you.

JULIÁN: I'm going crazy with all these questions!

THERAPIST: I understand. I feel that you're feeling overwhelmed. You know, the perk of the sandtray technique is that you don't have to speak too much, or at least not until you are ready and want to.

JULIÁN: I don't have to talk to these dolls? I thought I'd have to put them there and you'd start asking questions...

THERAPIST: No, you didn't give me time to explain, you went off like a spring! (*Jokingly and smiling*)

JULIÁN: (*Already calmer and responding slightly to the smile. I notice that we have connected for the first time*) Well, I could do it, but not today. I feel screwed, I'm going crazy, I had some drama with the educator last night...

THERAPIST: If you are not feeling well, it's best to put it off to another day. No rush. Next session? If you want, I'll explain more in detail how it works. Oh! And another day, how about you tell me how you are? So, I don't have to play fortune teller (*smiling kindly*). If we both do our part, we could understand each other and I will also learn to "read" you and sense how you feel. I think this was good, it's interesting for me, I got to know you a little more today and I'll learn to adapt a bit more.

JULIÁN: Damn...! I thought you were going to throw me out in the street when I yelled at you and told you about the f**king sandtray!

THERAPIST: I don't like being talked to and yelled at like that, like you. Nobody likes it. But I'm not going to kick you out of here. You can get angry if you want, anything but hit me and insult me (*we laugh at the same time*). I'm here to help you and anger was your way of telling me that you needed something, and you didn't know how to express it in another way. We will be able to learn to express things, even if you sometimes lose control, like everyone else.

Figure 3.1 Julián was encouraged to make his first sandtray!

JULIÁN: (*Surprised with my response but relaxed*) It's true that I get in trouble because I can't control myself… (*Connects with it and gets overwhelmed again*) Let's leave it for today, okay?

THERAPIST: Thanks for asking. We'll take it slow. It's okay that it's difficult, it's painful to connect with it. (*Silence*) I agree. Until next week. I'll be waiting for you.

JULIÁN: (*With a cigarette already in his mouth*): Ok. Thank you, José Luis (*first time he expressed something positive*).

From this session, I noticed that we made a significant leap in the therapeutic relationship, as Julián started trusting me. We began to connect better with each other. Not only should conflicts in the therapeutic relationship not be avoided, but they are a profound change and improvement booster, and offer opportunities for repair—in the here and now of therapy—of past traumatic relational experiences recorded in memory.

Working methodologies with the sandtray technique in trauma therapy

As we have already briefly pointed out in the previous paragraphs, there are two methodologies for approaching and working with the sandtray technique. It is necessary to use and combine both in order to help and treat patient problems thoroughly. But first and foremost, each patient must be offered the methodology that best suits their personality, characteristics and attachment profile. There are patients who initially reject the directive approach, but in more advanced phases of therapy, with more resources, security and confidence, they tend to open up.

For Pearson and Wilson (2001), when the patient is offered a free (nondirective) approach to the sandtray, the work has less impact on the symbolic level (although the box can also be explored at this level, if we delve in the personal and universal sphere). On the contrary, when we propose the directive approach to the patient, i.e., by suggesting a topic, we are (although not exclusively) trying to help them elaborate an event (indirectly or directly related to it), thus appealing to the symbolic world.

Ana María Gómez (2013) in her book *EMDR therapy and adjunct approaches with children* develops the two methodologies of approaching the sandtray.

Non-directive methodology

Gómez (2013) states that the use of symbols and figures used in the sandtray space allows the patient to get that distance they often need to explore

Table 3.1 List of topics that can be proposed to the patient using a directive work methodology with the sandtray technique (proposed by the Southern Sandtray Institute)

School-age children
Family.
Friends from school.
A regular day in your life.
One side of the tray will be the best in your world. The other part, the worst in your world.
One side of the tray represents you when you feel happy. The other side when you feel sad.
Your favourite things.
The thing that scares you the most in your world.
How do you calm down when you feel nervous?
What do you want to do when you grow up?
Teenagers
Your life timeline.
Your happiest memory.
The obstacles you have faced.
Your ideal future.
What love means to you.
The most important thing in your life.
Commitment.
Your daily routine.
What you see when you look in the mirror.
Your worst nightmare (both imagined and actual dream)
Adults
Your hope about the outcome of therapy.
One of your biggest fights.
Your earliest childhood memory.
Your saddest childhood memory (Combine it with your happiest childhood memory).
What guilt means to you.
How others can show you their love.
What do you do to be able to get back on your feet after facing adversity.
The best possible day.
Your family (children, partner, parents...).
What would you want to do if today was the last day of your life?
Your thoughts when you put your feet on the ground when you get up in the morning.
Three things you can do tomorrow to feel better.
What your father or mother would say about you if they made a sandtray.
Your best attribute or characteristic.
How would your life be different if [...] was not in your life? (Depression, divorce...).
Your feelings while lying in bed at night.
Your favourite part about your life.

experiences that can be overwhelming. In addition, it facilitates access to early preverbal memories about trauma and adversity.

Highly traumatised and dysregulated children and adults may begin to build -with great distance from those memories- by creating a world in a nondirective way. It is the best way in any case, and the safest for all patients to start.

This is the reason that the comprehensive evaluation of every patient before starting treatment is so important: to know how to implement the techniques, specifically the sandtray. When we find ourselves with children and adults who lack resources, the non-directive sandtray can capture the internal conflicts of the child, providing them with the highest level of distance (Gómez, 2013).

Using this methodology, we invite the patient to let themselves go and allow the figures to choose him or "call" them without too much thinking. Then we move on to the co-exploration phase (or if it is a child, possibly play phase). The questions aimed at co-exploring the scene are formulated from within it, related to the characters of the world in the sand. We proceed with the basic questions if it is their first sandtray. Depending on whether we are working on the goals of Block I, II or III, we can use the sandtray with questions and different levels of depth. We will develop this in the following sections.

The non-directive methodology can be used in all three blocks and for some people it may be the best way to work with this technique, because some patients always require this distance to be able to process the traumatic contents and overwhelming emotional problems. Specifically, this can occur—although not exclusively—with patients with few psychological resources and very damaged by trauma from an early age. We'll decide later if a more directive approach can be tried, if we think it is beneficial to the client. But if the patient refuses, we should not think that our intervention is incorrect or inappropriate. We are adapting the technique to the patient! It is very likely that they do not have the resources to work otherwise.

Directive methodology: work focused on therapeutic goals

With this approach, patient and therapist choose to explicitly and directly work on a therapeutic goal (or an aspect of it) with the sandtray. In the non-directive methodology, goals are also worked on, but indirectly; that is, we can also spot the patient's problems reflected in them. We must keep in mind that the goals, in Barudy and Dantagnan's methodology (2010; 2014), are always agreed on with the patient, after the comprehensive evaluation and before the intervention phase, written on a sheet of paper and kept in folder. We have already explained in previous paragraphs what *directive* means, so I will not expand further on how we apply this concept here.

There are two strategies: when the patient's *self* is indirectly present in the created scene and when it is directly present. We are going to illustrate them in the following paragraphs (Gómez, 2013).

The patient's *self* is indirectly present in the sandtray work

Patients (especially children) can hardly work in therapy exclusively with words, face to face, with an adult therapeutic scheme or framework. This is not child psychotherapy! And even with many adults it is not always possible to proceed that way.

We need to provide our patients (especially if they are children) with tools through which they can express themselves, adapted to their age and level of maturity. We have already discussed several times that sticking to verbal therapy can retraumatise minors. We must also include other elements such as emotions and body sensations (Ogden et al., 2009), and do so through safer means adapted to the child's level of development, like play therapy, the sandtray, drawing, etc. (Barudy and Dantagnan, 2012; Cornejo, 2008; 2014; West, 1995).

Barudy and Dantagnan's training in systemic-child trauma therapy offers an evaluation and understanding model and a very large number of intervention techniques, adapted to children with different types of abuse trauma.

The patient's *self* is indirectly present in the sandtray. In this methodology, there is less distance, we would be at an intermediate level with respect to traumatic memories (Gómez, 2013). In order to work with the patient in this way, we must deal with more psychological resources (cognitive and emotional) and be comfortable with this approach.

We may ask the patient to represent a concern, topic or generic difficulty of those among the therapeutic goals. For example, a child agreed with me to make a tray about impatience, something that they usually feel as a problem, which sometimes leads them to not knowing how to wait and to having conflicts with people or spending all their pocket money.

Then, we proceed in the co-exploration of the world with the basic questions, and we can, even if the child or the adult patient is prepared, and it is useful and beneficial for them, complete the said co-exploration with the questions referring to the personal or archetypal sphere.

A generic topic that is related to the patient's reason for consultation. For example, we asked Socrates, an 11-year-old boy whose father died suddenly, to make a sandtray with *loss* as a general theme.

The patient, working on a specific therapeutic goal, gets stuck, blocks, does not know how to express and explain themselves, does not understand what is happening to them, is confused, has mixed feelings... An invitation to use the sandtray technique can be made to represent what they want or feel in relation to this and then carry on with all phases, co-exploring to the level that is tolerated and well processed by the patient.

For this reason, we usually choose to work with this methodology in Block II and especially in Block III. The sandtray tool is a great tool for dealing with and reconstructing traumatic life stories and elaborating them on a symbolic level.

The questions for Block II or III can be specific depending on what we are working on. We will see it later in this book.

The patient's *self* is directly present in the sandtray work

In this therapeutic strategy the patient's *self* is explicitly present. It is the shortest distance from the content because it represents a specific traumatic or adverse event, or said content causes physical and mental suffering. And/or it entails personal, emotional, painful relationship problems (Gómez, 2013).

If the person can access the traumatic contents of the memory in this way and has the psychological resources to work with this methodology, the patient can be invited to proceed in this way (as, for example, the Juan Ramón case that we explain in chapter for). In any case, although the *self* is directly present in the sandtray, there is still a distance from the trauma because the miniature represents it. It represents the patient and verbalises through it and from within the created world. This is the fascinating thing about this technique, and what makes it safe!

The patient is told: *"Choose a miniature that represents you and do what you want about..."* (*...the accident you had; when you felt rejected by your friends at school when you were eight years old; when they told you that you were adopted, when you go to foster care...).*

Before this, patient and therapist have represented the life history line in a graph, recording the adverse or traumatic events experienced by the patient, in chronological order and evaluating the emotional impact that they generate in the present. We tend to proceed from the least disturbing to the most disturbing. Probably the patient will need our security and previously to learn some regulation techniques.

The Southern Sandtray Institute proposes a list of themes from which the patient can create a sandtray. The client must be able to work at this level, have the capacity to carry out a reflective function and present abilities to regulate their emotions, living together in a safe and protected environment.

The themes can be proposed to the person in an indirect way or by requesting the present *self* (miniature that represents them in the world in the sand).

In their book *Sandplay and symbol work*, Pearson and Wilson (2001), also illustrate different themes for working with the sandtray in a directive manner, although their proposal focuses more on the symbolic plane, above all on the personal and universal sphere. This approach to the sandtray -as we have already mentioned- is more appropriate for patients with reflective capacity, learned emotional regulation skills, a protective context and a desire to change and deepen aspects of the *self* (see Table 3.1).

There are minors and adults who present complex trauma and attachment disorders -not all, obviously, but a significant number- who cannot work at this level because their brain/mind is not integrated, and they need to start from Block I. Some will be able to reach a more symbolic work—more typical of Block III—and others may not. *"Patients do what they can with what they have"*, say Barudy and Dantagnan (2014) referring to the limitations that some people have in their brain/mind due to traumatic damage.

Note

1 The concept of neuroception is different from that of perception. In perception, there is a component of cognitive assessment. Neuroception, on the other hand, is about sensations and emotions that are experienced below the level of consciousness and that are recorded in implicit memory during the preverbal stage, before the appearance of language. It transmits the message that the anticipated expectation and consequence related to the attachment figures is safe. (Ogden & Fisher, 2016) It is a kind of hunch, of feeling that the child feels in their body and in their skin, that these people are going to give him security and empathic care.

References

Barudy, J. & Dantagnan, M. (2010). *Los desafíos invisibles de ser madre o padre. Manual de evaluación de las competencias y la resiliencia parental.* Barcelona: Gedisa.

Barudy, J. & Dantagnan, M. (2012). *La fiesta mágica y realista de la resiliencia infantil: Manual y técnicas terapéuticas para apoyar y promover la resiliencia de los niños, niñas y adolescentes.* Barcelona: Gedisa.

Barudy, J. & Dantagnan, M. (2014). *La trauma-terapia sistémica aplicada a los niños, niñas y adolescentes afectados por traumas. Un modelo basado en los buenos tratos y la promoción de la resiliencia.* Powerpoint presentado en el marco del Diplomado en trauma terapia infantil sistémica. Bilbao: Documento no publicado.

Bromberg, P. (2011). *The shadow of the tsunami and the growth of the relational mind.* New York: Routledge, Taylor & Francis Group.

Cornejo, L. (2008). *Manual de terapia infantil gestáltica.* Bilbao: Desclée de Brouwer.

Cornejo, L. (2014). *Manual de terapia gestáltica aplicada a los adolescentes.* Bilbao: Desclée de Brouwer.

Gómez, A.M. (2013). *EMDR and adjunct approaches with children. Complex trauma, attachment and dissociation.* New York: Springer Publishing Company.

Ogden, P., Minton, K. & Pain, C. (2009). *El trauma y el cuerpo. Un modelo sensoriomotriz de psicoterapia.* Bilbao: Desclée de Brouwer.

Ogden, P. & Fisher, J. (2016). *Psicoterapia sensoriomotriz. Intervenciones para el trauma y el apego.* Bilbao: Desclée de Brouwer.

Pearson, M. & Wilson, H. (2001). *Sandplay & symbol work.* Melbourne: Australian Council for Educational Research.

Porges, S.W. (2011). *The polyvagal theory: neurophysiological foundations of emotions, attachment, communication and self-regulation.* New York: W.W. Norton & Company.

Schore, A. (2003). *Affect Dysregulation and disorders of the self.* London: W.W. Norton & Company.

Siegel, D.J. (2007). *La mente en desarrollo. Cómo interactúan las relaciones y el cerebro para modelar nuestro ser.* Bilbao: Desclée de Brouwer.

West, J. (1995). *Terapia de juego centrada en el niño.* México: Manual Moderno.

Chapter 4

The sandtray technique: The work of identification, expression and emotional regulation (Block I)

We apply the Three-block Model of Psychotherapy designed by Barudy and Dantagnan with minors, but it can also be adapted to psychotherapy with adults. The same neurosequential order (adaptable) in the intervention must be followed with these (Perry et al., 2013).

Barudy and Dantagnan's psychotherapy can be used with all patients. With those who present a sufficiently secure attachment and an integrated personality, with psychological resources to work with and have a supportive family environment and context, with one or a few traumatic events, the psychotherapy approach designed by these authors offers excellent results in a very short time.

For patients who have suffered abandonment, mistreatment and sexual abuse and present psychological damage, the Model of Barudy and Dantagnan turns out to be very suitable and offers very good results: its principle of application of neurosequential order, comprehensive evaluation, level of involvement of the therapist, the domains affected in the patients and on which they act (trauma, attachment and development) and the three blocks of treatment with their objectives and techniques make it a model **adapted to patients damaged by mistreatment.** However, the duration of psychotherapy is usually longer with these, and it is characterised by advances and setbacks, with more complex challenges to face[1].

With patients who present significant challenges, the treatment is more complex, and it is also more difficult for them to bond with the therapist and with psychotherapy. They are minors and adults who present chronic and severe trauma. They manifest disorganised attachment strategies and have moderate to severe symptoms of dissociation. The presence of comorbidity (the coexistence of two or more pathologies) is high, as well as self-destructive behaviours and the absence of regulatory tactics. The family system is—or has been—often chaotic and highly deregulated or absent (Gómez, 2013). They present a reactive attachment disorder (Gonzalo, 2015; Cantero & Lafuente, 2010), mood disorders and dissociative disorders (Gómez, 2013; Baita, 2015; Silberg, 2019). Fragmentation, permanent emotionality and psychophysiological dysregulation, together with

DOI: 10.4324/9781003359111-4

a very narrow tolerance window for emotions are normally prevalent, especially in minors (Gómez, 2013).

The presence of internal resources and memory networks that contain adaptive and congruent information about the *self* and others are absent or scarce. For this reason, managing the therapeutic relationship is also more delicate, since they can prematurely abandon psychotherapy. Sometimes, in the context of psychotherapy, transference/countertransference relationships are made, i.e., when the unconscious conflicts that both (patient and therapist) experienced in their childhood are enacted (Wallin, 2012).

After the comprehensive evaluation phase, which will inform us on how the patient is specifically affected in terms of trauma, attachment and development, we normally have to start working with block I, as it is necessary **to generate psychological resources of self-regulation and stabilisation of the symptoms.** These patients function according to *lower-order action systems* (Steele et al., 2008) because the trauma has left them *fixed* in a survival position. It is difficult for them to efficiently use the superior cortical neural pathways and, specifically, the fronto-limbic circuit (Schore, 2003) responsible for the proper management of impulses and emotions. For this reason, before considering other objectives for which the patient may not be prepared, we will focus on achieving the goals of Block I.

We work with various techniques—for the different objectives of this block—designed by Barudy and Dantagnan (2014) and enriched, over the years, by the therapists of the APEGA Network, who have made significant contributions. It is not the purpose of this book to explain these techniques, but to explain how I use the sandtray in this first block to work on some objectives for which we consider this technique appropriate.

The sandtray for Block I can be a very useful and valuable tool, and we have to adapt it to the patient's profile and to the goals we pursue in this block. **Specifically, we usually use the sandtray to develop expressive skills and adequate modulation of emotions.** The first sandtray helps us to assess the capacity of the minor or adult to identify, express and regulate emotions. There will be patients who will surprise us with their first tray because the technique, by itself, enhances this capacity. Others, on the other hand, will require specific and special interventions because they present a deficit in this sense. The sandtrays that we can make in this block will be used to work on this. We will see how to do it next.

Connect emotionally with the patient through the sandtray technique

The sandtray technique is, as we have been stating throughout this book, a genuine therapeutic experience. Complex trauma patients may not approach trauma in all balanced modes (emotional, physical and intellectual) due to psychophysiological dysregulation of their nervous system (Steele et al.,

2008). Some patients may do it in an intellectualised way, devoid of emotional and sensory connection (those with features of an avoidant attachment); and others, on the contrary, can become hyperactivated and move within excessive emotionality (patients who present traits of an anxious-ambivalent attachment). Patients who manifest characteristics of disorganised attachment will present both modes in an inconsistent manner.

As we discussed describing the psychotherapy model of Barudy and Dantagnan (2005; 2010), **attachment is one of the three domains to evaluate in our patients.**

It is very important to know the types of attachment in order to properly treat each patient and adapt the techniques to them, including the sandtray. It is not the purpose of this book to focus on attachment and its disorders. To learn more, we recommend consulting the following authors, among others: Barudy and Dantagnan, 2005 and 2010; Bowlby, 1989; Cantero and Lafuente, 2010; Holmes, 2009; Liotti, 2006; Marrone and Diamond, 2001; Ogden et al., 2009 and 2016; Siegel, 2011; Schore, 2003; Wallin, 2012.

What we now want to underline are two central concepts in attachment theory:

The internal working model (Bowlby, 1989). For the first year of life, the baby develops a mental scheme regarding the bond of attachment that it has developed with the main caregiver—based on relational experiences with the latter—which contains information that allows them to evaluate the quality of that bond, the expectation on the caregiver's behaviour and also to assess themselves. The attachment bond can be secure and insecure (and within it: insecure avoidant or insecure anxious-ambivalent) (Ainsworth et al., 1978).

Attachment and regulation. This field of research has been developed, among other authors, by Schore (2003) who argues that the primary function of the attachment figure is to achieve an affective synchrony between baby and caregiver that allows the infant to develop emotional regulation skills that are based in the right hemisphere of the brain, which is predominant during the first two years of life. A competent caregiver who is capable of effectively modulating the child emotionally, connecting and synchronising with them is necessary for the hemisphere to grow properly.

As psychotherapists who apply the sandtray technique, what we have to keep in mind with patients who present various types of traumatic experiences (abuse, abandonment, prolonged neglect during the first two years of life), is that they can easily lose their ability to regulate their emotions. They had these experiences at a time when the foundations of future socio-emotional competence are developing, and their window of emotional tolerance is very narrow.

However, the sandtray technique is a safe means of expression because the psychic content and the emotionality associated with it are represented in concrete physical forms that can be manipulated, touched, named... and be spoken about. Let us remember that the patient speaks of the created world and from within it. They do not talk about themselves. This offers, per se, enough distance to remember and deal with emotional problems and traumatic content without losing control and suffering. If we do not ask too many questions or delve into personal matters too much too fast, it is in the co-exploration phase when the technique can be overwhelming or generate rejection in people with a tendency towards hypoactivation (avoidant) or hyperactivation (anxious-ambivalent). As professionals, we want the patient to stay connected with us and their world in the sand by letting emotions flow (experiencing moderate-slightly high levels of activation); but we have to prevent it from breaking relational harmony. Why? Because if the levels of activation are too high or low, the person cannot process the experience with the sandtray; they prevent balance in the three modes of experience (intellectual, emotional and physical-sensory). So, it is no longer therapeutic because information is not processed (Ogden et al., 2009; Ogden & Fisher, 2016).

The sandtray technique allows the connection with the *self* because it is relaxing (manipulating the figures with the hands, touching the sand). Respecting the work pace of each patient, whether they have to or don't have to go through all the phases, and avoiding direction, enhances the patient's connection with the sandtray. In addition, there is an essential ingredient to achieve connection with the client and keep them regulated within moderate-high activation levels: the presence of the therapist and empathic receptivity throughout the process. Finally, the last element is understanding the conscious meaning of the symbols and bridging with real life. Some patients will need to work with the tray a bit longer to get here. And some may never get here. But the unconscious working with the symbols helps patients with their problems too. We can see it in the case of this child called Ron.

Ron is a six-year-old boy who recently lost his father due to cancer. The child saw his father's entire process of deterioration until, unfortunately, the father died. The mother was so anguished throughout the process that she could not tell the child what was happening to his father. Subsequently, the duel influenced so that the mother was not available for the child. Ron developed aggressive behaviours, anger and disobedience towards the mother. The sandtrays reflected the guilt that the child felt for the death of the father, with violent scenes, where there were no container and protective symbols.

Traumatherapy consisted of assessing and support maternal competence to promote the resilience. She went to the mourning group and had the support of her brothers too. This was essential for the mother to regain her abilities to re-establish an emotional connection and reassure the child through the exercise of calm authority. This combined work of support for the mother and free sessions with the sandtray where the child represented his initially violent worlds, made him evolve towards the understanding and integration of affective and container elements, from unconscious symbolic work, without the need for make the child aware of it. The trauma of the loss of the father drew her safely by playing with the sandbox.

Initially, we will connect much more and more safely with **patients with avoidant attachment traits** if we enhance the relationship with the created world. We will go through joint explorations that include safe questions such as the ones we have collected in Tables 4.1 and 4.2. We can take advantage of silence to reflect.

As a second step—in the first sandtray, or in the following—we can try to **mirror the patient** and give back to them the way we felt their communication with the figures was like, like an echo that resonates in both, enhancing the emotional capacity of the patients, which is underdeveloped in some. The questions that reflect the patient like a mirror and favour the development of their emotional capacity are collected in Table 4.1 We must bear in mind that we reflect what the patient expresses about the figures or items, but we are returning these feelings from the perspective of the figures or asking the patient to imagine that they are one of those figures.

Mirroring the emotional world of the figures and returning that reflection to the patient, making them feel as if it was their own, highlighting it, favours the development of **mentalisation** (realising that they have their own mind with emotions and thoughts that are their own), often damaged in patients with complex trauma and attachment disorders. Also, doing it from within the world itself and from the character or miniature is not invasive at all (Fonagy et al., 2005)

Table 4.1 Expressions that the therapist can use to mirror back to the patient the emotions and internal states of the figures and items in the exploration of the created world

If the patient says that a figure feels (or does, or says, or thinks...) in a certain way...	...we mirror ("let go, stay in that experience...") using their words.
If the patient says that a figure feels (or does, or says, or thinks...) in a certain way... Or tells us what is happening in the world...	...we mirror ("allow yourself to recognise the importance of this")
Idem	...we mirror ("let's see if you can learn more about this")
Idem	...we mirror ("be aware of how it resonates in your body")
Idem	...we mirror ("see if you can experience this more deeply")
Idem	...we mirror ("allow yourself to open to this")
Idem	...we mirror ("see if you can allow yourself to value this experience more deeply")
Idem	...we mirror ("let it be and see what happens")

Adapted from Rae, 2013.

The mirroring must be done respecting **the patient's pace**. Stay silent so that they take their time and go deeper into the experience.

Later, we can consider the co-exploration of the meanings and formulate the questions listed in Tables 1.3 and 1.4. As long as it is useful for the patient at that moment to enter the personal and universal spheres.

With clients with avoidant traits, if the therapist is too direct, invasive and moves too soon from the sandtray world into the client's real world, the client may respond with defences (denying, projecting, disengaging and even downplaying the technique). We must then repair and restore relational harmony. The patient may have their good reasons for shutting down. We must validate their feelings or reactions and be receptive.

For some patients with avoidant traits or with inhibited attachment disorder, limiting co-exploration to the world inside the tray and working with metaphors, playing inside it if they are children, makes them feel safe and may be the only way to work with them. Inhibited attachment disorder is a severe alteration in the establishment of the attachment bond in childhood that the world in the sandtray mediates. It is like a channel of relationship and work, without having to reach to the exploration of the personal and universal spheres between patient and therapist. On the other hand, other avoidant children and adults will gain in security components and will allow us to build bridges with the personal and universal sphere.

Patients with anxious-ambivalent traits. We can, with some of them, favour the connection with the world they have created and also with us as therapists. The patient with anxious-ambivalent traits is more involved in the therapeutic relationship because they maximise the emotional component, so they will probably start working with the technique from the emotional and sensory mode at the expense of the intellectual (just the opposite of avoidant patients).

The questions listed in Tables 1.1 and 1.2 (in Chapter 1) will also be safe for them, when we walk them through the joint exploration of the world.

Mirroring what the figure can feel or think from within their world to the patient and checking how this affects the patient is usually a good experience for the child or patient with anxious-ambivalent traits. The risk is that if the mirroring is done too intensely, the patient may hyperactivate by connecting with a traumatic content stored in their implicit memory (they are very reactive patients on an emotional level, with a tendency to anxiety) and go beyond their emotional window of tolerance. This could break relational harmony and teenagers with these traits may not want to do any more sandtrays, so we have to be very delicate and cautious.

The joint exploration of the world, building bridges between the sandtray and the patient's personal life or the universal realm must be done with caution, as they can connect with a feeling of intense **vulnerability**. These people almost always feel insecure about the availability of the other and their emotionally intense responses are ways of asking for help. Exploration that focuses on cognitive understanding that makes sense of their chaotic emotional world is useful for them, especially allowing them to see their resources in the created world (some create dramatic scenes full of fear, danger and risk, but they also tend to introduce elements such as policemen, superheroes, doctors, nurses, that should be supported and explore how they can be applied to their real life). They tend to feel helpless rather than seeing their resources and how to strengthen them.

When playing in the sandtray we can connect with minors by reflecting and emotionally amplifying their game in a natural way, without looking into interpretations (West, 1995).

Patients with disorganised attachment traits. They do not manifest an organised attachment strategy, but rather manifestations of the other two in an incoherent way. We must bear in mind that these people have suffered intense experiences of fear and anguish with their caregivers (the people they bonded with are those who harmed them), from which they have not been able to escape and the strategy they developed to survive was dissociation (Liotti, 2006).

Therefore, we must proceed with the utmost care and caution with them. The questions in Tables 4.1 and 4.2 are the most appropriate because they are the most indirect and safe. Exploring the personal and universal spheres must be done when the patient is organising and structuring towards one of the other types of attachment and we are sure that this co-exploration will be truly useful. When they present severe damage, it is best to just work with the sandtray, limiting ourselves to the metaphors contained in it without building bridges with real life.

We should not be afraid that relational harmony can be broken. This can happen because as human, we are not perfect, and we make mistakes. This is an opportunity to learn and improve our work. Most importantly, this harmony can be restored through the qualities of the therapist, including empathetic receptivity. Knowing the patient well, upon making a good comprehensive evaluation, respecting their pace, adapting to their possibilities and proceeding slowly, carefully, as when handling a physical wound, will powerfully help the process of co-exploration to be useful, safe and lived by the patient within moderately high levels of emotional activation and without getting overwhelmed. The patient's verbal responses, their behaviour, their body language will let us know if they are prepared or not to continue.

How to know one's emotions and to express them with the sandtray technique

In order to help patients to get to know and express their emotions, we mainly have two methodologies: non-directive and directive. Depending on the patient's attachment style and other variables such as personality traits, life context, psychological resources that he/she presents, mentalisation capacity, etc., we will determine which approach is safest to use. As we have already mentioned, the best way to start is the non-directive methodology: make a free sandtray.

Non-directive methodology to get to know and express emotions

There are patients whose deficits are a consequence of repeated traumas, especially abandonment, which implies a prolonged absence from the attachment figure, and therefore their capacity to know and express emotions is limited. They need emotional psychoeducation. This objective from Block I can be tackled with the sandtray. It's surprising and fascinating to notice the difference it makes for some patients to express their emotions through the figures in the tray than face to face with the therapist, when they get stuck and are unable to answer. Others, on the other hand, will struggle even more but we can help them develop these skills with the sandtray in a safer, more creative, fun way.

We give the patient the instructions that we have collected in Chapter 1, and they can do whatever they want with their sandtray.

Later, after the silent contemplation phase of the sandtray, when we sit down with the patient to co-explore the world created by them, we adapt the questions in Table 4.1 to help them to get to know and express their emotions.

We can also mirror the patient using the strategies presented in Table 4.1, but only if they talk. Most patients tend to start telling us about their world, but sometimes we will have to encourage them to do so by adapting the questions collected in Table 1.2 (in Chapter 1) in this way:

Table 4.2 Question to get to know and express emotions with adults and children (for age ten and over)

"Tell me about…"	"…what they are doing, thinking, feeling…" (it is less invasive to ask what the miniatures are doing first and then move on to what they feel)
"Let's take a moment…"	"…to talk about the little bird on the tree. How does it feel?"
"I wonder…"	"…how the woman inside the house feels: angry, sad, happy, nervous…? (We should say this with such a tone that the patient feels that we are asking a question, not suggesting options. We mention four basic emotions, especially with minors who have a lot of trouble identifying them. We do it slowly, giving the person time to think and connect)
"Let's learn more…"	"… about the boy's feelings when the monster is about to attack him"
"Let's learn more…"	"…about the soldier's anger"
"Let's stay a little longer…"	"…to see what we can learn about the dog's happiness"

We can see an example from a clinic session (transcriptions):

Knowing and expressing emotions using sandtray

Let's examine a example in real life: Socrates is an 11-year-old boy whose father died in a car accident. Very intelligent, rational, scientific, with avoidant attachment traits, he was very defensive with me initially. We must keep

Figure 4.1 The two parts of the sand world of Socrates

in mind that he felt threatened because he thought we were going to talk about his father, to whom he was very close, and this made him feel over-whelmed. When he saw the sandtray on the shelf, he immediately connected with it and asked me what it was for. I explained it to him briefly and he asked if he could make a sand world.

In Figure 4.1 we see the world he created. This is how I helped him develop his emotional skills, which needed to be enhanced before he could tackle grief work. Also, the experience served us both to connect with each other throughout the world.

THERAPIST: Do you want to tell me what is going on in this world?
SOCRATES: These (*pointing to the characters in the background*) are defending the forest. They are going to face these others (*pointing to monsters*) and want to win the battle. Those from here (*right of the photo, next to the trees*) are fighting to save the forest. They are in conflict with the monsters, who want to destroy the forest.
THERAPIST: I wonder how those who defend the forest might feel. (*Silence*)
SOCRATES: They feel confident... (*Silence*)
THERAPIST: Let's learn more about this confidence they feel.
SOCRATES: (*Stays silent for a while*) They think they are going to win... There has to be a fight...
THERAPIST: Tell me how the others feel.
SOCRATES: (*Silence*) Also confident in victory. They are very powerful...
THERAPIST: Are they related to each other?
SOCRATES: No. Some want the world one way and others another. There is no middle ground.
THERAPIST: Let's stay a little longer to learn about this...
SOCRATES: They can't understand each other and have to fight. Sometimes aggressiveness is the only way out... (*Shows signs of wanting to finish*) Shall we play?
THERAPIST: Sure. But you have to tell me which figures I'm going to handle, what you want me to do, and what the end will be.
SOCRATES: Okay.

The characters on the left are nightmare symbols, perhaps alluding to a more aggressive *self*-state that was unleashed as a result of the father's death (Socrates had behavioural problems). The other part on the right represents perhaps the usual, the contained, more rational, showing admirable ethical values that can later be explored as an archetype (ecology). We write all this down, but we do not tell the patient at this stage. We hope to enter Block II or III and at a time that we think will be useful to them.

Directive methodology to get to know and express emotions

Within this methodology, we can use the sandtray in two ways to help the patient to learn about or express themselves on an emotional level.

The patient does not know how to express what they feel about a problem, symptom or issue. They may get stuck. They seem confused, doubtful, struggling within. We can suggest approaching the shelf and let themselves get carried away by that feeling of uncertainty and allow the miniatures to choose them to place them on the surface of the shelf sand without too much thinking.

Then, after the silent contemplation phase, we proceed to co-explore the sandtray using the previous questions (those adapted from Table 4.1) and/or those from Table 4.2.

Working with basic emotions (joy, fear, sadness and anger) or with more elaborate ones (tranquillity, surprise, disgust, anxiety) we can suggest elaborating the sandtray by letting themselves get carried away by words. For example: *"Would you like to make a sandtray about joy, hope, fear…?"* We think it is more suitable for adults and for children over ten years of age with preserved development. It can be way too difficult for certain minors. Others will not be able to speak at all. When this happens, we let them know it may not be a good day for this practice or the right approach for them. We restore relational harmony, if necessary.

When we work with the sandtray in Block I of trauma therapy, with the aim of promoting knowledge and expression of emotions and especially when we employ the directive methodology, we involve the left hemisphere from the beginning of the application of the technique. In this case, this is exactly the purpose the sandtray; for now, we are not working on the resilient elaboration or reintegration of traumatic contents.

Emotional regulation with the sandtray technique

Identifying, expressing and regulating emotions is often a process that requires simultaneous learning. We can teach a patient to recognise what they feel, give it a name, express it and realise where in the body they feel it and how intense it is, and provide them with a regulation technique, especially if they are very intense emotions and more difficult to manage, like rage.

We have already discussed that we have to take special precautions and care with children and adults who present complex trauma, disorganised attachment and dissociative symptoms (Gómez, 2013). They can become psycho-physiologically deregulated more easily and go over the window of emotional tolerance, especially while doing the joint exploration; specifically, when the distance from the traumatic event is intermediate, or the patient's *self* is directly present in the scene, or when we carry out the joint exploration of the personal and universal spheres and the person becomes hyperactive or overly underactive. Patients with a secure attachment (or with an *"imperfect but still secure attachment"*, as stated by Ogden and Fisher, 2016) and with greater regulatory capacity, on the other hand, are better able within the window of emotional tolerance.

Emotional regulation skills are worked on, reviewed and used throughout therapy, and are specifically necessary when we work on Block II and especially III (when representing traumatic content and dealing with life history).

Therefore, in addition to the sandtray technique, we usually teach the patient **mindfulness skills**. Mindfulness means paying full attention to the contents of the mind in the present moment (psychic activity: emotions, thoughts, memories, sensations…), observing them as such (they are a part of the experience of the mind, it is not me), with curiosity, openness, acceptance and without judging if they should happen or not (Siegel, 2011).

Mindfulness skills allow the patient to restore awareness in the present. This is very important when a traumatic past memory is activated: if the patient is processing it, directing attention to the present moment helps to integrate it (Gómez, 2013). It is as if one eye were in the past and the other in the present (Siegel, 2011). In addition, learning to observe an emotion as such, as part of the activity of the mind, accepting it without fighting against it, favours its regulation. The frontal lobe is strengthened when mindfulness skills are regularly practiced, an area of the brain responsible for regulating emotions and impulses (Siegel, 2011).

The simplest mindfulness exercise is to train the patient to attentively observe the emotion with openness and curiosity—because it always says something about oneself—like a detective, encouraging them not to fight against it *("What You Resist, Persists—What You Accept, Transforms"*, a Buddhist principle that applies to mindfulness); allowing themselves to feel it without judging, perceiving it as an emotion and accepting it because it is part of them. In the same way, some patients find it helpful to focus their attention on the breath, carefully observing the cycle of inhalation and exhalation. To learn about mindfulness for adults, see Germer and Simón, 2011; and for mindfulness applied to children, see Greenland, 2013. But like any technique, it requires education, training and practice.

These skills can be transferred—and combined after training—to work with the sandtray technique. We are going to see an example that will serve to illustrate how knowledge, expression and regulation of emotions can be worked on with an adolescent patient.

Juan Ramón was able to express and modulate his painful emotions about a bullying experience suffered in the past using a directive approach with the sandtray.

Juan Ramón is a 19-year-old boy who was bullied in high school for several years. Suffering from back problems and a limp, he was ridiculed by some youngsters for two years. He regained normal body posture after an operation. Upon returning to the institute, none of his usual classmates and friends were interested in how the operation had gone. He felt alone and felt by no one. From then on, he decided to study his last year of high school on his

Figure 4.2 Juan Ramón used storm trooper miniatures to represent his self directly in this sandtray

own and refused to go out or interact with kids his age, spending long hours playing video games, at the risk of developing an addiction.

After several sandtrays with a non-directive methodology, we agreed to focus on the traumatic memory he had of high school. He agreed to make a world with the self present, choosing a miniature to represent him (see Figure 4.2). Before then, he had been trained in mindfulness (breathing and observing his inner world, with full attention and without judging). It was his first sandtray with his self present, he was ready for it, and we tried to address the personal sphere as well, i.e., bridging between the world in the sand and his real life. It is a sandtray to work on in Block III, but the patient needs to use emotional regulation skills in all blocks. Therefore, it will serve to illustrate how the patient can be helped to stay within the tolerance range for emotions when working with the sandtray.

THERAPIST: Do you want to tell me about this world?

JUAN RAMÓN: Sure, I don't mind. This one inside here (*the white soldier inside the central gate*) is the one that represents me.

THERAPIST: What are you going to name him?

JUAN RAMÓN: Storm-trooper. It's like inside... a... (*his voice is shaking*) box, like... I don't understand, like... in different groups (*I represented them like this, grouped, through these miniatures; some are from the Empire— referring to the characters of the Star Wars saga—and others are from the Republic, let's say*). A bit like different groups, like he doesn't trust them, he's involved... well, they mess with him... (*he's activated but he doesn't go over his limits. He's a boy who isn't very skilled with verbal language.*)

THERAPIST: Can we find out more about Storm-trooper's feelings when they mess with him?

JUAN RAMÓN: (*Does not answer the question*) These (*giving their backs to Storm-trooper*) don't really mess with him. These that are closer to him (*the miniatures located in front and behind Storm-trooper*) get involved

Figure 4.3 Juan Ramón rebuilt the world in the tray and made changes

less and as they move away; they get more involved. Now that I see it I think I should have put them differently.

THERAPIST: You can do that, if you want.

JUAN RAMÓN: Yes, I am going to change them.

And he rebuilt the world placing it as we see it in Figure 4.3.

JUAN RAMÓN: That's better. The more we move (*towards the bottom*), the more they mess with him. There were many groups and Storm-trooper felt alone, like he didn't have much confidence because he was moving away for different reasons, and he didn't trust the friends he had since primary school. And in secondary school, they did some stuff that let him down. Those who are further away, messed with him from primary school and carried on the secondary school...

THERAPIST: What did they do exactly?

JUAN RAMÓN: He's afraid... They insulted him, they hid things from him to make fun of him, they threw an orange at him, they stuck a lollipop on his hair, they called him names for his body...

THERAPIST: Let's learn more about Storm-trooper's feelings.

JUAN RAMÓN: He feels hurt because even his closest friends let him down...

THERAPIST: Stay a little longer to see what you can learn about Storm-trooper's feelings.

(You can see from his body that he's feeling tense and agitated.)

JUAN RAMÓN: Angry, sad, mad... (*emphasising the word*)

(Silence)

JUAN RAMÓN: Sad to see that you trusted those people and they have abandoned you. And angry (*with a lot of anger in his voice*) because they have a-ban-do-ned you.

THERAPIST: I feel that it is painful for Storm-trooper to feel abandoned... But now it's over, you are here, with me, in the session, you're safe now.

(Depressed)

THERAPIST: Can we make a bridge between this world in the sand and the real world? But first, how do you feel?

JUAN RAMÓN: I'm struggling...

THERAPIST: Is this a good time to build this bridge? Can you go on?

JUAN RAMÓN: Yes, yes, I can continue but I'll struggle a bit...

THERAPIST: Can you breathe a little—remember your safety circle? (*A technique we had previously tried that implies remembering people he is close*

to, connecting with them, evoking them, feeling their presence and safety.)
You need to regulate your emotions, is it too much for you?

JUAN RAMÓN: Yes, I want to breathe a little.

THERAPIST: You know how to do it. Come on.

JUAN RAMÓN: Yes, yes…

(Pause)

THERAPIST: (*When Juan Ramón is more emotionally regulated and has got back into the window of emotional tolerance*): These are memories of hard experiences. You're releasing the emotions connected to them, but the events are over, it's just a memory. Storm-trooper has recorded it inside of him.

JUAN RAMÓN: But it's still hard for me…

THERAPIST: Of course. It's hard and painful. But you're being really brave working on it, this is how you'll overcome it. Shall we continue?

JUAN RAMÓN: Yes, I can go on now.

THERAPIST: This is good time to make a summary of what happened here, before leaving the world.

JUAN RAMÓN: I made the world with Storm-trooper representing me. I noticed it was better that way because it reflected better what I had gone through.

THERAPIST: Then you have learned about Storm-trooper's feelings when he was mistreated and even those who he thought were his best friends abandoned him.

JUAN RAMON: Yes.

THERAPIST: Now let's see how we can bridge between the world of the sand-tray and the real world. (*I start looking out of the world.*) How can you use what you learned today in the sandtray in the outside world?

JUAN RAMÓN: I realise that I don't trust people, that it's hard for me to open up…

THERAPIST: Of course, you don't. After the painful experience you've gone through, it's normal that you find it hard to trust people.

(Silence)

THERAPIST: What do you need?

JUAN RAMÓN: I think I need to approach people with more trust, see that they're not like the ones who mistreated me… that it doesn't have to happen again… But it's hard for me…

THERAPIST: Exactly. That's very good. When this traumatic memory of the past is integrated into the present and you can see the people and the world around you with the eyes of the present, you'll trust more.

JUAN RAMÓN: Yes, I hope so.

(Silence and pause)

THERAPIST: Well, our session is about to end. You've done so well! Shall we take a photography to explore the world together again and discover new things that might help?

JUAN RAMON: Yes.

Six months into therapy, Juan Ramón began to feel in a better mood, to express his emotions more, to appear less distant and closed in on himself. He wanted to meet the kids he connected with online to play video games.

Note

1 The negative effects of psychic trauma can reappear in people at times of intense stress or in critical periods of life; sometimes, the interaction between person and negative life context can influence a new relapse because traumas make the personality much more vulnerable, less integrated and consistent in periods of stress. In certain cases, the damage that people's psyche (mind and brain) has suffered marks their personality and requires them to undergo a resilient reconstruction process that continues throughout their lives. People can be transformed thanks to the beneficial influence of other human beings; they can be remade from a trauma. But in some cases, the psychic wounds suffered were so powerful and at such critical ages that they reopen again. In these cases, being aware of them, knowing how to take care of oneself and seeking the support of a psychosocial network allows them to recover again. For this reason, resilience is not a goal but a constant process of personal reconstruction throughout life, a social reconstruction that always requires others to give us bond and meaning (Cyrulnik, 2003).

References

Ainsworth, M., Blehar, M., Waters, E. & Wall, S. (1978). *Patterns of Attachment.* Hillsdale, NJ: Erlbaum.

Baita, S. (2015). *Rompecabezas: una guía introductoria a la disociación infantil.* Buenos Aires.

Barudy, J. & Dantagnan, M. (2005). *Los buenos tratos a la infancia. Parentalidad, apego y resiliencia.* Barcelona: Gedisa.

Barudy, J. & Dantagnan, M. (2010). *Los desafíos invisibles de ser madre o padre. Manual de evaluación de las competencias y la resiliencia parental.* Barcelona: Gedisa.

Barudy, J. & Dantagnan, M. (2014). *La trauma-terapia sistémica aplicada a los niños, niñas y adolescentes afectados por traumas. Un modelo basado en los buenos tratos y la promoción de la resiliencia.* Powerpoint presentado en el marco del Diplomado en trauma terapia infantil sistémica. Bilbao: Documento no publicado.

Bowlby, J. (1989). *Una base segura: aplicaciones clínicas de la teoría del apego.* Barcelona: Paidos Ibérica.

Cantero, M.J. & Lafuente, M.J. (2010). *Vinculaciones afectivas: apego, amistad y amor.* Madrid: Pirámide.

Cyrulnik, B. (2003). *El murmullo de los fantasmas.* Barcelona: Gedisa.

Fonagy, P.; Gergely, G.; Jurist, E. & Target, M. (2005). *Affect Regulation, mentalization, and the development of self.* New York: Other Press.

Germer, C. & Simón, V. (2013). *Aprender a practicar mindfulness.* Barcelona: Sello editorial.

Gómez, A.M. (2013). *EMDR and adjunct approaches with children. Complex trauma, attachment and dissociation.* New York: Springer Publishing Company.

Gonzalo, J.L. (2015). *Vincúlate. Relaciones reparadoras del vínculo en menores adoptados y acogidos.* Bilbao: Desclée de Brouwer.

González, A. & Mosquera, D. (2012). *EMDR y disociación. El abordaje progresivo.* Madrid: Ediciones Pleyades.

Greenland, S.K. (2013). *El niño atento. Mindfulness para ayudar a tu hijo a ser más feliz, amable y compasivo.* Bilbao: Desclée de Brouwer.

Holmes, J. (2009). *Teoría del apego y psicoterapia. En busca de la base segura.* Bilbao: Desclée de Brouwer.

Liotti, G. (2006). A model of dissociation based on attachment theory and research. *Journal of Trauma & Dissociation,* 7(4), 55–73.

Marrone, M. & Diamond, N. (2001). *La teoría del apego. Un enfoque actual.* Barcelona: Psimática.

Ogden, P.; Minton, K. & Pain, C. (2009). *El trauma y el cuerpo. Un modelo sensoriomotriz de psicoterapia.* Bilbao: Desclée de Brouwer.

Ogden, P. & Fisher, J. (2016). *Psicoterapia sensoriomotriz. Intervenciones para el trauma y el apego.* Bilbao: Desclée de Brouwer.

Perry, B., Brandt, K., Seligman, S. & Tronick, E. (2013). *Infant and early childhood mental health: core concepts and clinical practice.* United Kingdom: American Psychiatric Publishing.

Rae, R. (2013). *Sandtray: Playing to heal, recover and grow.* Plymouth: Jason Aronson.

Schore, A. (2003). *Affect Dysregulation and disorders of the self.* London: W.W. Norton & Company.

Siegel, D. (2011). *Mindsight: La nueva ciencia de la transformación personal.* Barcelona: Paidós Ibérica.

Silberg, J. (2019). *El niño superviviente. Curar el trauma del desarrollo y la disociación.* Bilbao: Desclée de Brouwer.

Steele, K., Nijenhuis, E. & Van der Hart, O. (2008). *El yo atormentado: la disociación estructural y el tratamiento de la traumatización crónica.* Bilbao: Desclée de Brouwer.

Wallin, D. (2012). *El apego en psicoterapia.* Bilbao: Desclée de Brouwer.

West, J. (1995). *Terapia de juego centrada en el niño.* México: Manual Moderno.

Chapter 5

The sandtray technique to work on empowerment (Block II)

Block II of Barudy and Dantagnan's specialised psychotherapy model for trauma treatment, attachment disorders and alterations in the development, as we referred to in Chapter 2, is entitled Empowerment[1].

Victims of prolonged mistreatment, abuse, neglect or abandonment and who present damage in the domains of trauma and attachment have experienced multiple situations where they did not have control, they felt helpless, humiliated, harassed... They are permanently hypervigilant (a neuroception of danger, in the terminology of Porges, 2011). When a stimulus from the present activates a traumatic memory due to its symbolic similarity with events suffered in the past, the brain-mind of people with chronic trauma reacts for survival because it has not integrated that these events are in the past. Fight or flight response and freezing are two examples of typical reactions to neuroception of danger in people suffering from chronic trauma. The non-integrated experiences registered in the emotional memory are timeless and can be triggered by certain stimuli.

Therefore, among other purposes, the reader can consult chapter two of this book to remember the goals of Block II, in this block we work so that the patient can recover their lost power (which is why Maryorie Dantagnan called this block using the word empowerment), the feeling of control on their own life, and learn to see their current life context as safe and protective.

A wide range of therapeutic techniques are used in this block. The sandtray is one of them because it is a useful and valuable tool to contribute to empowerment. By representing the traumatic contents of life story into concrete physical forms, we ensure that they did not just "happen", but rather the patients **take ownership** of them by **reconstructing** them. And this is possible because both cerebral hemispheres intervene when working with this technique: the verbal capacity of the left hemisphere helps the patient to shape, transform, elaborate the unconscious psychic contents (emotions, sensations...) that are based in the right hemisphere. Preverbal traumas, prior to the appearance of language, are recorded in the latter. The sandtray can access them in the creation phase through "*thinking in images*" (Rae, 2013) and co-operate with the left hemisphere to process these traumatic contents

DOI: 10.4324/9781003359111-5

Table 5.1 The questions we can ask to co-explore the empowerment with the patients

"Tell me about…"	Any empowering aspect the patient has already mentioned. For example: "…the strength of the tiger; the doctor who heals; the policeman who watches; the soldiers who kill the beasts; the safe place…" There are hundreds of possibilities.
"Let's take a moment (to see) …"	When we want to stimulate executive functions, e.g. "…what would happen if the child crossed the lake full of crocodiles; what happens when the guy at the checkout gets carried away with impatience; what the consequences for the thief are; what would happen if it went another way; If he didn't steal…" Encourage superior mental actions that help the child to reflect on the consequences of the characters' actions or their decisions.
"I wonder…"	For example, for projection of the future: "…if two opposing sides will achieve peace; if the children will know how to get back safely through the dark path; if someone will come to save children from drowning; if someone will take care of these children; if you can see a better future; if things will go well; if there are other alternatives…"
"Let's learn more…"	(About specific traumatic aspects symbolised in the sand) Examples: "… about that ogre that terrorises those people; that dragon that wants to attack; that armed ninja getting into the family home; that child who's always alone and sad; that abandoned house; that man who scares people; that place you don't want to go to; that enchanted forest; that rough sea; that sinking ship; the shark that kills the whole family; the drowning family…" The possibilities are endless.
"Let's learn more…"	(About resilient aspects that emerge in the box and represented by scenes and symbols, even of an archetypal nature) Examples: "… about that holy place; that God; that force; that policeman, judge, soldier, doctor, nurse…; that green place full of flowers; that energy, power, lightning, superpowers; superheroes and resilient and counter-resisting characteristics of evil forces or enemies; that sorcerer who heals everyone…", etc.

during the co-exploration phase. Obviously, this is facilitated by the presence of professionals capable of creating restorative experiences with this therapeutic approach. To learn more about trauma and preverbal memory, see Schore (2003).

As we have already mentioned in previous paragraphs, we have used the sandtray technique to treat the following goals from Block II: stimulate executive functions, address the internal working model and learn alternative strategies to deal with mental actions derived from trauma.

The work methodologies are, namely, non-directive and directive. Both provide positive results. As always, we advise to use the one that best suits our patient, their characteristics and how much they have been affected by trauma and attachment domains. **The strategy we usually pick for patients who are heavily affected by trauma is the non-directive approach.**

The questions we can ask when we work on this block are in Table 5.1, they are adapted from Rae (2013). The patient is more prepared to let their resilient resources emerge, as the bond with the therapist is strengthened. There is more trust and a feeling of safety, their creative and healing potential can be brought to light, along with the aspects we can take advantage of to empower the child or the adult. Through their stories, narratives, scenes we will provide resilient expressions and we will reflect them with emotional resonance.

This capacity for empowerment can arise in every **protected victim**. The brain has the natural resources to be able to heal (Shapiro, 2013) when it encounters a technique as healing as the sandtray and a facilitating therapist.

We are going to see **two examples** of sandtray work towards two of the goals from **Block II** entitled **empowerment**. In the first one, using a non-directive methodology, a patient addresses their insecure attachment with her mother (working on the internal work model, a concept of Bowlby, 1989). In the second, a twelve-year-old boy agrees to make a sandtray to focus on a therapeutic goal. What worries him is his impatience and the consequences of not stopping to think and foresee the consequences of his actions (work mental actions derived from trauma).

Work empowerment with the sandtray through the non-directive methodology

How to work attachment working model through sandtray

Let's examine the case of Genoveva working with sandtray. She is 30 years old and goes to psychotherapy to deal with episodes of anxiety. These happen especially in interpersonal relationships, with people who have authority or people she feels close to she is afraid that making a mistake could lead her to lose their affection and their positive attitude towards her. After a few months of therapy sessions where we worked with mindfulness to learn to regulate emotions, especially her anxiety, and after developing a strong therapeutic bond, we agreed to work with the sandtray technique.

Figure 5.1 Genoveva preferred the non-directive methodology (it was her first sandtray, after all) and represented the scene without being given any theme or instruction

She had a solid and secure bond with me as well as psychological resources and was able to regulate her emotions. Therefore, I decided to do a complete therapy session in order to help her associate episodes of anxiety deriving from criticism with the insecure anxious-ambivalent bond that she had developed in her relationship with her mother in childhood. This would have empowered her in the present.

Although her sandtray may seem sparse in miniatures and items, it was very rich in the way she accessed it (from sensory and emotional experiences as well). She expressed emotionality in her tone and was very connected to the tray and me at this level (see Figure 5.1)

GENOVEVA: (*After a long phase of silence and contemplation of the scene*): I feel a lump in my throat...

THERAPIST: Do you need to regulate emotions?

GENOVEVA: No, I can continue.

THERAPIST: How was making the tray?

GENOVEVA: I have a lot of imagination but it's hard for me. I don't know what happens to me, but I always struggle participating in imaginative games...

THERAPIST: You know that nothing could go wrong, this is not like other games.

GENOVEVA: What I mean is it's difficult for me to pull it out... (*NB: Patients who are aware of what they are doing, connect emotionally and when they see the psychic content visually captured, they increase awareness and enter the emotional and sensory mode. This is positive if it is done within the window of emotional tolerance.*)

THERAPIST: I understand. It's hard to show it.

GENOVEVA: Yes, it's hard to show this thing I've done.

THERAPIST: I'm here with you. Do you want us to co-explore together?

GENOVEVA: Yes, yes. It's better if you ask me questions.

(We sit)

THERAPIST: Okay. I noticed that the first thing you placed was this miniature...

GENOVEVA: Yes, Heidi. (*Her voice shakes*) For Innocence.

THERAPIST: Let's stay a little longer to feel Heidi's innocence.

GENOVEVA: (*Confirms*) I haven't seen much of the series, but she makes me think of innocence. A girl who felt alone, abandoned, who was taken away from her grandfather without much explanation...

THERAPIST: Let's stay a little longer with Heidi's feeling.

GENOVEVA: (*Cries*) I get emotional... I feel the lump in my throat...

THERAPIST: Let that feeling stay, observe that lump with curiosity and acceptance, let it be. It's an emotion asking to be taken care of, not be fought against, as we do with mindfulness.

GENOVEVA: (*Sits in the meditating posture and breathes for a couple of minutes*) I chose her because she is a girl. I chose her and took her.

THERAPIST: Sure, no permission is needed (*smiling*).

GENOVEVA: (*Smiling*) Yes, I know...

THERAPIST: Tell me about Heidi's feelings in that sand world.

GENOVEVA: (*Snorting*) Well... I don't really know how to describe it, I don't know...

(Silence)

GENOVEVA: Perhaps she's waiting for something to happen...

THERAPIST: Tell me more about this wait.

GENOVEVA: ...she's waiting for someone to tell her something...

(Silence)

THERAPIST: I wonder if what Heidi feels is a tense expectation or a calm expectation.

GENOVEVA: It's rather tense...

THERAPIST: Let's learn more about it.

GENOVEVA: It is a tense expectation that they will tell you something. About her behaviour, something negative...

THERAPIST: Is that a worried expectation that Heidi feels there?

GENOVEVA: It's rather nervous, anxious... She's got anxiety, waiting for them to say something rather bad.

THERAPIST: I imagine it must be hard for Heidi. Can you tell me if there is something in particular that she is afraid of?

GENOVEVA: (*Silence*) Well, maybe she's telling them about an experience she had in class afraid and she's afraid that they might (cries) contradict her.

THERAPIST: I wonder if she feels judged...

GENOVEVA: They don't put themselves in her shoes...

THERAPIST: As if they didn't validate what she's going through?

GENOVEVA: (*Long silence. She breathes, stops crying and calms down a bit. She doesn't get overwhelmed*) Yes, that's it.

THERAPIST: Can we say more about Heidi?

GENOVEVA: No. That's it.

THERAPIST: Shall we continue? Then there's that miniature...

GENOVEVA: I wanted a dark-haired woman but I couldn't find it (*laughs*). She gives the impression that she's nice, that she's saying hello, she has a good face, I don't know... she looks good. At first. She says hello and... everything's fine. But then (*long pause, then she gets emotional again*) there's that snake behind...

THERAPIST: (*After a silence*) I feel that it is very painful for Heidi.

GENOVEVA: Yes, it is...

(After some silence)

GENOVEVA: She bothers Heidi. Constantly. "Not this", "This won't work", "This is not good", "You don't know how to do this"...

THERAPIST: I wonder if it's a metaphor for showing a nice face but hiding a snake behind it, which can come out and hurt. It's the representation of the damage it can do, it's unexpected.

GENOVEVA: (*emphasising*) Exactly. You don't know where it's going to come out from. Snakes can be alright if you do what they want, but when you do something, they don't like, they bite you. They attack you.

THERAPIST: Tell me more about the woman.

GENOVEVA: I don't know… (*Silence*) To tell you the truth, you never know…

THERAPIST: I wonder if she is aware that she can bite like snakes.

GENOVEVA: (*Categorically*) I don't think so. She's not aware of what she's doing.

Figure 5.2 Genoveva made this change in her sandtray world

(Pause and silence. Genoveva seems calmer now)

THERAPIST: Would this world need anything?
GENOVEVA: I don't know... (*she thinks in silence*) Some support, someone who is between her and the snake. Or something...
THERAPIST: Stay a little longer to feel that something.
GENOVEVA: What she would really need is the distance.
THERAPIST: Is it good for her?
GENOVEVA: Yes.
THERAPIST: Note how good it is for Heidi to take that distance (*strengthening empowerment*)

(Silence)

THERAPIST: Would you like the world to have that distance?
GENOVEVA: Yes, yes. I want Heidi to get some distance.

(long pause)

THERAPIST: And now?
GENOVEVA: She's off the field.
THERAPIST: How is Heidi feeling now?
GENOVEVA: Relieved.
THERAPIST: Stay a little longer noticing that relief.
GENOVEVA: The lady doesn't understand the distance, she experiences it as rejection. She doesn't understand what she has done or what she hasn't done. She asks for explanations...
THERAPIST: (*Silence*) Let's spend a little more time on this.
GENOVEVA: She doesn't understand that Heidi hasn't felt loved or valued. Few good words have ever come out of her mouth. She's received so many complaints, so much criticism...

(long silence)

THERAPIST: I feel that it is very painful for Heidi not to feel valued and loved. But she is not to blame. This is due to the woman's emotional disability, not to Heidi. She's just a girl.

(long pause)

GENOVEVA: Yes, that's true.
THERAPIST: Do you want to say something else or is this a good time to summarise what we have experienced exploring the tray together and leaving the world of sand?

GENOVEVA: It is a good time to finish and summarise.

(We do the summary of the session with the sandtray and we prepare to build a bridge between it and her real life. We enter the personal realm and so now I begin to speak to her directing my gaze to her face and not to the world, to favour this transition.)

THERAPIST: Is there a way to take care of this form of awareness that you have acquired here in your daily life? You seem aware of many things, which is positive.

GENOVEVA: Yes, I could find a connection between the tray and the fact that I worry about losing people's affection.

THERAPIST: Go ahead.

GENOVEVA: I may repeat this pattern with the people I work, with that fear of making a mistake, or that they think I made a mistake. I feel unappreciated and think the snake's going to come out. Something along these lines.

THERAPIST: Do you mean that you re-enact something from your childhood? Something about your relationship with your mother?

GENOVEVA: Yes, yes, yes... I can see it.

THERAPIST: There, in the everyday life, with your bosses or other people you love, you must see yourself from the present, trust in your abilities and realise that making mistakes is human, and that their affection has nothing to do with being perfect.

GENOVEVA: My bosses, my friends... they are not looking at me with the same eyes as my mother.

THERAPIST: (Nodding) Very good! Well done! This can help you to look at it from a different perspective and not reproduce that anxious bond with other people.

GENOVEVA: Yes, it makes sense.

THERAPIST: You may be getting the same lump in your throat...

GENOVEVA: No, no, no... I feel calm, relieved, I realise now that what upsets me might come from there. I don't have to take it like I used to, like when I was little.

THERAPIST: Very good. Do you see it?

GENOVEVA: Yes.

THERAPIST: Do you notice it anywhere on the body?

GENOVEVA: In the gut.

(Here we apply bilateral stimulation to reinforce this awareness and this positive feeling.)

THERAPIST: (After finishing the stimulation) How are you?

GENOVEVA: Very good.

THERAPIST: Can you think of any other way you could apply the sandray world to your life?

GENOVEVA: (*Thinks*) No, not right now.

THERAPIST: We can come back to it another day.

GENOVEVA: Yes.

THERAPIST: Ready to be able to wrap up the session with the sandtray? Excellent work, Genoveva.

GENOVEVA: Thank you.

(We took a picture of the sandtray and returned everything to its place.)

Work on empowerment with the sandtray through the directive methodology

How to learn alternative strategies to mental actions derived from trauma

Let's examine a case study taken from psychotherapeutic practice. Juan Mari is a 12-year-old boy in permanent foster care since he was one year old. At the age of nine, his foster parents requested psychological treatment after the reappearance of his biological mother. She had handed over Juan Mari's custody to public administration as she was not able to take care of him. It was necessary to address the integration of this new event with this child, help him in the meetings with his biological mother and work on his life story, giving meaning to foster care.

Juan Mari is a minor who has a tendency to emotional and psychophysio-logical dysregulation, making it very difficult for him to manage his emotions and impulses. For this reason, he struggles to carry out school tasks and follow rules and norms to co-exist and relate appropriately with his peers. His behaviour, well-being and psychological adjustment are quite satisfactory in the foster family, who collaborate and devote themselves to trying to repair that first year of life in which Juan Mari suffered emotional abandonment. They were also very supportive when his mother unexpectedly appeared in his life, causing a lot of confusion. He is happy, but also scared because he loves his foster family and feels that he cannot find his place.

Juan Mari feels frustrated when he is not rewarded by his foster family. A non-integrated *ego state* is activated within him, entails a complete mental action of a lower order: he steals significant amounts of money and spends it without any control, showing everyone what he has bought (trinkets, cards...). Then, when he is confronted with the theft, it is not hard for him to admit it. He feels sad, guilty, affected by negative feelings and accepts the consequences from his foster family.

This is not so much a behavioural problem that seeks to break the rules of coexistence and mutual respect, although it could lead to it in the long term.

Figure 5.3 Letting himself be carried away by the word impatience as a general theme, Juan Mari built this scene

They are mental actions derived from early abandonment trauma (Steele et al., 2008): *a state of the self* (Gómez, 2013) close to infantile dissociation (Baita, 2015), implying painful emotions deriving from affective deficiencies recorded in the implicit memory. These are acted out in the present through stimuli that can provide feelings of euphoria, which this patient obtains by stealing. The neural pathways of the lower brain are activated and in a state of emotional dysregulation it is not possible to activate awareness, stop, think, make choices by anticipating the consequences of your actions and monitor your behaviour to manage frustration, which are mental actions of a higher order. Trauma affects the brain because under these deprived states, these higher neural networks were not stimulated. Juan Mari learned from an early age to react and instead of responding, as befits some people who have had to fight to survive since birth. As he says about himself: *"I am very impatient"*.

We worked with Juan Mari in Block I for a long time (a year and a half). It was in Block II when, by mutual agreement, we decided to tackle what he calls impatience through the sandtray. In this block, we also started to recognise the impact of early trauma in his life and empower him (see Figure 5.3)

THERAPIST: (*After the contemplation phase of the sandtray scene*) Do you want to tell me about your world in the sandtray?

(Juan Mari is not very skilled with words, so he cannot work at this level using all his cognitive potential.)

JUAN MARI: This (*pointing to the policeman next to the plane, on the edge of the tray*) tells the boy in front of him that he is going to give him a plane.

THERAPIST: (*Nods head*) Yes, yes.

JUAN MARI: Security (that's what the policeman is called) told him that he had to wait a week to get the plane because it was being repaired. This one (*the representation of Anger in the movie* Inside Out) appears and says to the boy: "Oh, well, I'm going to get it!". Suddenly, the alarm sounds (*opens the doors of the police car in the background and an alarm sounds*). "Who's there? Who's there?", says the policeman. He wakes up and realises that his plane got stolen. And that's it.

THERAPIST: And the truck and the miniature next to it?

JUAN MARI: They are for decoration.

THERAPIST: Tell me more about the one that can't wait...

JUAN MARI: He gets the plane because he can't wait.

THERAPIST: Yes. The planes and the tank?

JUAN MARI: They are also decorative.

THERAPIST: Do they have something to do with the rest?

JUAN MARI: No (*categorically*).

THERAPIST: What will happen next?

JUAN MARI: They will catch him and punish him.

THERAPIST: I wonder how this one feel (the boy, the one who steals the plane).

JUAN MARI: I don't know... (*Silence*) Furious...

THERAPIST: Let's stay on this a little longer. What else can he feel, or say...?

JUAN MARI: He's got problems. He doesn't know how to wait; he can be impatient...

THERAPIST: I wonder if he can learn to do things differently.

JUAN MARI: It is very difficult for him, but if they help him, he might be able to.

THERAPIST: How can they help him? Tell me more about that.

JUAN MARI: He has to stop this guy (*referring to the miniature from the movie* Inside Out, *Anger*) He's very strong, he pushes him...

THERAPIST: What could he do to stop him?

JUAN MARI: Listen to the security...

THERAPIST: If he did listen to them, what would the consequence be?

JUAN MARI: Very different! He would not steal, and they would not punish him, because they can take him to jail if he steals...

THERAPIST: What does this one need? (*The miniature that steals*)

JUAN MARI: (*Thinks*) He needs to stop him, like, to reassure him (pointing to Anger). If he's calm, he won't steal.

THERAPIST: We are going to focus on this and dedicate some time to feeling that calm that stops this one, let's concentrate. (*Pause for a minute*) How are you?

JUAN MARI: I'm better.

THERAPIST: Is there anything this world needs?

JUAN MARI: No, no... (*Shows signs of wanting to finish*)

THERAPIST: Okay. As we have to take a picture of the sandtray now, we can look at it again another day, if that's okay with you. I would like to know how he can listen to the security and how they can help him. Not now though, you look a little tired, aren't you?

JUAN MARI: Yes, I want to finish now, I want us to play with the remote-control car, otherwise we won't have time.

THERAPIST: It's true! Well, before we take a picture, we do a brief summary of what we have done since we started with the sandtray.

JUAN MARI: Good.

It is possible that as professionals many more questions and issues arise that we would like to clarify. But the child has had enough: it takes mental effort to represent an emotional problem that causes him a lot of pain and dominates him, despite keeping intermediate distance using the miniatures. Surely, we will wonder about the meaning of the planes, the tank, the truck… but we cannot carry on yet. Not everything can be understood and that is normal. They might be aggressive symbols, or on the contrary, symbols of control and help over that *self-state* that is unleashed. We do not know yet. But what is truly important is that the child has represented the scene, has worked with it to the best of his ability, we have adapted to his level and cognitive possibilities, he has stayed within the limits of emotional tolerance and relational harmony has been preserved. Later on, if it's helpful for Juan Mari (let's not forget this) we can co-explore the sandtray again to learn more, and we able to build a bridge and relate it to his life story in the future. But this is a lot of work for a single session. In addition, Juan Mari informed us about a voice that speaks to him under that deregulated state, encouraging him to steal. Therefore, he has given us an invaluable clue to carefully work on that state in therapy with him. He has also told us that he can get over it if he gets help. This implies networking with the context of the child's family and school life and agreeing among all how to help Juan Mari, how to regulate him and control him and what consequences can be taught.

Note

1 Generically, by "empowering" we mean the increase in authority and power of the individual over the resources and decisions that affect their life.

References

Baita, S. (2015). *Rompecabezas: una guía introductoria a la disociación infantil*. Buenos Aires.

Bowlby, J. (1989). *Una base segura: aplicaciones clínicas de la teoría del apego*. Barcelona: Paidos Ibérica.

Gómez, A.M. (2013). *EMDR and adjunct approaches with children. Complex trauma, attachment and dissociation.* New York: Springer Publishing Company.

Porges, S.W. (2011). *The polyvagal theory: neurophysiological foundations of emotions, attachment, communication and self-regulation.* New York: W.W. Norton & Company.

Rae, R. (2013). *Sandtray: Playing to heal, recover and grow.* Plymouth, UK: Jason Aronson.

Schore, A. (2003). *Affect Dysregulation and disorders of the self.* W.W. Norton & Company: London.

Shapiro, F. (2013). *Supera tu pasado.* Barcelona: Kairós.

Steele, K., Nijenhuis, E. & Van der Hart, O. (2008). *El yo atormentado: la disociación estructural y el tratamiento de la traumatización crónica.* Bilbao: Desclée de Brouwer.

Chapter 6

The sandtray technique to work on the resilience reintegration of traumatic contents and psychological elaboration of the life story (Block III)

When we think of the word *trauma*, what normally comes to mind is a shock suffered after a specific event that poses a threat to our physical and mental integrity: an earthquake, a car accident, an assault... But today, the concept of trauma has extended: it also encompasses experiences and events of an inter-personal nature, that is, when a human being suffers the damage done by another human being, even in the context of an affective relationship and bond—couples, children and parents, work, peer relationships, etc. Jorge Barudy, neuropsychiatrist and family psychotherapist was one of the pioneers in research and in recognising victims of experiences such as abuse, mistreat-ment, abandonment—what is sometimes called *proximal abandonment*: par-ents physically present but emotionally absent (Schore, 2003). It is a pain that many of them carry, or have carried silently, to the extent that it can be invi-sible. This explains the title given by my friend and professor Jorge Barudy to one of his reference books, *The invisible pain of childhood* (Barudy, 1998).

Trauma, as defined by the EMDR Spain Association on its website www.emdr-es.org, is *"a 'psychological wound' that can be caused by various situa-tions. For example, when we hear about trauma, we associate it with problems caused by major natural disasters or by human beings, such as wars, accidents, abuse, etc. Specialists call them Traumas with a "T" due to the great magni-tude of their causes. There is also another category of traumas with a "t", whose origin is related to facts (...) such as: lack of protection, humiliation, change of roles in the family, etc."*

The extent to which somebody can be affected by trauma also depends on the characteristics of the person, the social support networks available and that they can refer to, and the time when it occurred. If traumas with "t" occur in childhood, we must bear in mind that it is a period of greater vulnerability (especially between birth and three years of age, since the infant depends on adults and the security they provide for their well-being, adequate develop-ment and protection). In order to be able to integrate the trauma in one's life and develop in a healthy, resilient and resourceful way, the minor will need the support of at least one adult who is able meets their needs and believe in the child or adolescent (Barudy and Dantagnan, 2005; 2010).

DOI: 10.4324/9781003359111-6

It is in Block III of Barudy and Dantagnan's Traumatherapy Model (2014) that patients are approached with this arduous task of dealing with the traumatic contents they have suffered and are helped to reconstruct their harsh life stories. It takes a great deal of energy, security, support, and empathic receptivity from the therapist to contain the patient's emotional pain and the way it is being expressed. Children and adolescents tend to externalise this pain through symptoms of hyperactivation, behaviour, emotional instability (they can become emotionally deregulated again), inattention... Or through disconnection, inhibition, depression... All this implies working side by side with the child's parents or caregivers (competent), so that they provide the minor with containment, regulation, security and emotional support in this stage of work. In the same way, the **co-ordination work with the professionals** of the school centre—and with another adult that work with the child or adolescent—is very important, so that they can understand and give a different meaning to the symptomatology of the minor. Some patients get worse while dealing with traumatic content. It will be a transitional period which will lead the patient to reintegrate and relocate their traumatic experiences in their brain/mind and, consequently, improve their symptoms and to a greater emotional well-being. Metaphorically speaking, it is like untangling a skein full of knots, or to finding the exit of a labyrinth that you walked in for ages. Trauma often involves the repetition of the same emotional and behavioural patterns (Wallin, 2012).

Many of the child or adult patients who come to our consultation seeking psychological treatment have suffered multiple traumatic events -traumas with a "T" and with a "t"—and very hard life stories. The absence of attachment figures in childhood, suffering from hunger, being a victim of prolonged sexual abuse, domestic violence, war refugees, invalidation of their mind, abandonment, loss of parents... These are life events and situations—sometimes prolonged—that are potentially very dangerous for the brain/mind; they can deregulate it and generate physical and psychological disorders of all kinds. As referred to by the psychiatrist and psychotherapist -and a great reference in the field—Rafael Benito (2015; 2020) not only are abuse and neglect are associated with mental disorders, but also with multiple physical illnesses and a greater probability of contracting them in adult life.

For all these reasons, this Block III is quite a challenge for the patients and the professionals who are going to support help them through **resilient reintegration** (Maryorie Dantagnan took this denomination from Puig and Rubio, 2011). It is called *reintegration,* because the traumatic contents and the sense of *self* are reintegrated over time, i.e., they are incorporated into a biographical whole. It is *resilient,* because unsuspected resources and qualities emerge to cope, work through emotional pain and change one's view of oneself and what has been suffered in life, transforming oneself. They go from *guilty* to *living* (Barudy & Dantagnan, 2005). The person is rebuilt and reborn after feeling *dead in life* (as described by Cyrulnik, 2015; 2020).

Patients who can work this block deserve all our admiration and respect for their courage. *"Room of the brave"*, says a poster in the children's therapy rooms of the APEGA Network (Jorge Barudy and Maryorie Dantagnan's idea); they have a place, materials and resources adapted to their needs. It is this how we empower them and convey the message that they are brave for daring to carry out psychological therapy.

Not all minors or adults meet the necessary requirements and conditions to be able to work in this block. We insist that from our point of view, adults must have psychosocial support networks that support them after therapy sessions and must be protected. Block III is never addressed if the person does not live in a protected environment. In the case of minors, they must also be protected and have the support of at least one competent adult who can meet their needs and collaborates as a co-therapist in this work of resilient reintegration.

In addition, both adults and minors have had to learn psychological resources to regulate emotions (Block I techniques are revised again) and acquire the ability for psychological elaboration (which involves the cortex: this is why we are in Block III, according to the neurosequential logic of Barudy and Dantagnan's Model). There must be sufficient reflective capacity in the person to be able to work on traumatic contents and their life story. Therefore, especially with children, their level of maturity is important in order to be able of reprocessing the traumatic events. Moreover, they must be motivated in some way to do this work, they must also have an interest. Not all foster children and adolescents have this interest, so the *timing* is important, the moment that they want and need to do this work of reconstructing their life's stories.

For directive sandtrays, where work is explicitly done with the patient's *self*, as well as to make elaborate stories that integrate the left and right hemisphere, the most suitable age is, in my experience, around nine–ten years old. We have to take into account the overall degree of cognitive and emotional maturity, not their actual age, of course.

Some people need additional preparation strategies to work on traumatic content because they have complex trauma, disorganised attachment, and dissociative symptoms. They must follow a specific treatment program, as designed by Gómez (2013).

There are people who, due to various factors and circumstances, cannot access this block of work. *"They will have their good reasons"*, says Maryorie Dantagnan. And we think we should stick to this. It may not be the right time, or they might not be ready for it. We have to respect it because life may give them other opportunities to repair the trauma—or other therapeutic possibilities more suitable to them—in the future.

The sandtray is not the only technique we use in this block, but it is the *star* of the techniques. As we already know, working on traumatic content exclusively through talking—without introducing the sensory and emotional components—is not enough and sometimes retraumatising. The sandtray technique allows these contents to be addressed in a safe space and with less emotional pain. Its kinesthetic properties, transforming the psychic world into miniatures, the symbolic creation of this world (which can be touched, felt... and talked about) and the activation of thought in images that goes directly and delicately to the right hemisphere, which is also where traumatic wounds are recorded, especially those that occur in the pre-verbal stage, make this therapeutic approach a powerful, useful and valuable tool for working on trauma. As long as the therapist is a trained professional and a person with human qualities, with empathy and a history of attachment and integrated and elaborated life.

Prior to using the sandtray for this task, it is convenient to have made a **life history line** in which we chronologically record the main events from our patient's life that are not integrated and that generate emotional pain, both traumas with a "T" and the periods of life characterised by traumas with a "t", i.e., attachment or relational trauma. We then assess the extent to which the patient has been affected by trauma and proceed to its representation in the tray of sand from least to most disturbing.

In general, the methodology of choice when starting Block III is the non-directive one, since it is the safest. We begin by encouraging the patient to make a free tray that sometimes tends to capture the traumatic contents (see Genoveva's sandtray).

With children, the first sandtray that we make at the beginning of therapy will help us detect trauma indicators. We know that children will usually play in the sandtray (Dantagnan, 2015):

Table 6.1 Trauma indicators in children's sandtray scenes

Difficulty staying within the limits of the tray (external and internal limits)
Presence of more regressive game (which corresponds to previous phases of development)
Presence of disorganised scenes.
Fictional content with considerable aggressive elements (animals devouring others or people)
Catastrophic endings.
Use of evil figures, monsters, bad guys...
Wild animals versus domestic or harmless animals.
Inanimate worlds without vegetables.
Prisons, forts, weapons...
Seemingly random, meaningless choice of figures
Seemingly nonsensical, incoherent game.
Figures representing adults not offering protection, rescue or help to defenceless figures. Children's figures or puppies in danger.
Victimisation
Long punishments.
Negative events without resolution.
Idealised worlds.

Dantagnan, 2015

As for adults, if they meet the requirements—i.e., they have a supportive and helpful environment and have sufficient psychological resources—and are comfortable with the directive methodology, traumatic contents can be worked on with this approach.

If our patient is a child or a teenager with one or few traumatic events in their life history and many positive attachment experiences; or a minor who is equipped with great resilience or some positive early attachment experiences with at least one caregiver despite their trauma (Gómez, 2013), they may benefit from a directive approach.

However, we should always make our decision depending on the comprehensive evaluation, on how much the minor is affected by trauma, attachment and development, and on an exhaustive knowledge of them. As in Block II, we can progressively make use of both approaches—directive or non-directive—to work with minors.

The **questions** that we can use to co-explore the sandtrays with the adult patient (and minor, if they are mature enough to work like this) and help them elaborate the traumatic contents are those in Tables 1.1 and 1.2. If it is possible to explore the personal and universal spheres and build bridges between the sandtray and the subject's life, we will use the questions in Tables 1.3 and 1.4. However, we must always proceed with caution in this block and make sure to keep the patient within the window of emotional tolerance (with moderate levels of activation), because authors and experts in trauma agree that information is not processed outside this window and therefore, we cannot help the patient to integrate the traumatic we are treating (González and Mosquera, 2012; Porges, 2011; Ogden and Fisher, 2016; Schore, 2003; Steele et al., 2008)

Let us see how to use the sandtray in Block III from clinical practice, that is, both to represent and address traumatic content (in a non-directive and directive way) and to create the story of the life history of those people who need to reconstruct meaning and awareness of oneself over time.

The sandtray technique to represent traumatic content: the non-directive approach

Parental separation can be traumatic for children

We are thinking about children like José Joaquín. He is a ten-year-old boy undergoing psychological treatment for depressive symptoms and behavioural problems arisen as a result of the traumatic separation of his parents. The level of conflict between the two due to infidelity and economic issues was so serious that the minor ended up witnessing harsh scenes of fights, insults and aggression from the father on the mother. The parents separated when José Joaquín was five years old. After that, custody was given to his mother. His father initially fulfilled his legal commitments of support, contact and relationship with his son. But after meeting a new woman (who had children), the father moved to another country when José Joaquín was five years old. His father built a family with his new partner and since then, their relationship has been limited to sporadic online meetings. In addition, the father stopped providing financial child support, claiming it was too high.

José Joaquín feels abandoned by his father. He misses his father figure and watches his schoolmates being dropped off for training by their parents, go for a walk with them, do their homework together, playing together... He had mixed feelings towards his father: he sometimes idealised him and other times he demonised him (he knew from his mother that he had chosen not to pay child support). He felt sorry that his family was torn apart and drew crying broken hearts.

His relationship with his mother got considerably worse as she worked long hours to support the family (she has another older son, who is 16 years old) and was overwhelmed by the situation. She reacted to José Joaquín's behavioural problems (his complaints about his life and depressed attitude) with shouts and punishments, neglecting the empathy and affection that, along with a good dose of firmness, this child needed. A therapeutic intervention with the mother was necessary.

From the beginning, he was very interested and attracted by the miniatures, the tray, the sand, how I had got so many miniatures... Questions that many children who are fascinated by the technique usually ask.

Figure 6.1 José Joaquin was able to express the emotional pain that the separation and its traumatic consequences had caused him

It is used to express yourself. You feel "the call" of the miniatures, let yourself go and choose the ones you want, to do what you want in this sandtray. Nothing can be done wrong; you just have to try not to spill the sand outside. "Do you dare to make something?", I said.

"I do", he answered.

In a nondirective way, the child represented traumatic contents that were related to depressive symptoms. The sandtray, as we mentioned, has the power to delicately access the right hemisphere and symbolise its contents in a way that words—besides being inadequate to deal with such painful content—could never do.

It is a metaphor of how he lives and feels about family conflict, the emotional unavailability of the mother and the abandonment of the father. It is most definitely an allegory of depression but, fortunately, with a glimpse of hope.

We did a co-exploration with the questions that we have collected in Tables 1.1 and 1.2 (in Chapter 1) and we did not go on to co-explore it in depth, as it was the initial phase of the therapy. We did not have enough knowledge of José Joaquín to risk him going outside the window of emotional tolerance. First, it was necessary to work on emotional expression and regulation and build the therapeutic bond.

It is relatively common for children and adult patients to start their first sandtray by showing us and projecting many of the problems and conflicts that need to be addressed, using the non-directive approach. They feel comfortable, calm and safe to create; the unconscious contents are represented without resistance through the language of symbols (miniatures and items) and grammar (the sandtray). It is a good signal. However, the first time I rarely co-explore in depth (reaching the personal and universal realms). I prefer to assess their mentalisation skills first, as well as their emotional knowledge and expression. I usually put off this task to Block III, which is dealt with, as we already know, in the final stages of therapy.

This was what José Joaquín expressed verbally about his sandtray. He was sad during the joint exploration of the scene, thereby suggesting that he was also connecting with the experience in an emotional way (see Figure 6.1).

THERAPIST: Do you want to tell me about what you have represented here?

JOSÉ JOAQUÍN: It's about the Simpson family. They had gone on a boat ride (the one in the foreground of the photograph, only the front part is visible) even if the father knew that the weather would be bad. A storm broke and they fell into the water.

THERAPIST: What do the miniatures do?

JOSÉ JOAQUÍN: The father, the mother and the child are drowning. Every time there are bigger waves, and they can't take it anymore... They are going to die, and the mother covers her ears in terror...

THERAPIST: Tell me about the miniature on top of that thing that looks like a boat...

JOSÉ JOAQUÍN: He is the youngest child in the family. He has found an old boat and has been able to get on it. He can't do anything to help others...

THERAPIST: How does he feel?

JOSÉ JOAQUÍN: Everyone is scared because they know they could die. But the little one feels safer.

THERAPIST: Let's learn a little more about this.

(Silence)

JOSÉ JOAQUÍN: The waves are huge... Even the little one is going to be knocked down by a wave... Everyone will die... Drowned...

THERAPIST: You say that everyone will die, it's very hard and sad for them, isn't it?

JOSÉ JOAQUÍN: The little boy cries a lot... He also feels alone, with no one there, on top of that boat... He screams but no one hears him with the storm noise...

THERAPIST: I wonder if someone could come help them or they will definitely die.

(This question is always interesting to assess the degree of hopelessness, self-punitive and aggressive impulses in depressed patients and possibilities to explore resilient strengths)

JOSÉ JOAQUÍN: When everything seemed lost, a helicopter appeared flying over the area.

THERAPIST: How do they feel?

JOSÉ JOAQUÍN: Very happy, they can be saved.

THERAPIST: Is the boy on the boat happy?

JOSÉ JOAQUÍN: Yes, very happy, he doesn't want to die, he's still very young.

THERAPIST: Sure! Good thing they're going to save them! Stay a little longer to notice the happy feelings of the child of the world you have created.

(Silence)

JOSÉ JOAQUÍN: It's not his fault. His father insisted on doing what he shouldn't have done. He went out on the boat knowing that the weather would be bad, without listening to those who told him that it would be very bad and dangerous. But he always does what he wants and doesn't think about others.

THERAPIST: I imagine that must be painful for the child. But I think he's absolutely right to be angry because it's the older person who hasn't done things right and he has put their lives at risk.

We then closed the session with a summary and took the photograph. Later in the therapy, in Block III, we went back to explore the sandtray together and we built a bridge with what he lived in his family, being able to see the father's parental incompetence. We worked with him to figure out if his feelings before the separation were like those of that child: like drowning, loneliness, helplessness, vulnerability… In this case, resilience is represented by the helicopter. José Joaquín wanted to take the photo just at the moment the helicopter appeared. This helicopter is very hopeful, it suggests that there are resources in this child. The scene is very dynamic and clearly shows the dramatic situation of his family.

The intervention done with José Joaquín when co-exploring the sandtray was therapeutic although not treated in depth. He metaphorically represented traumatic content in a safe and free way, staying within the window of emotional tolerance and being able to release and develop feelings of control. In addition, it helped the therapist to realise the need for this child to be *saved* (i. e., to be seen, rescued, felt, validated: he is not to blame for what is happening, he is a victim) and he must work on all this with his mother. Finally, this first sandtray allowed us to learn that his emotional knowledge and expression of emotions are quite developed and that he could probably work with Block I and II.

The sandtray technique to represent traumatic content: the directive approach

The sandtray helps the patient to express what words cannot, because the mind is stuck

Let's examine the experience of Sigfrido, a 15-year-old of South American origin and a victim of severe emotional abuse, who was adopted by his parents when he was five years old. His early childhood was marked by the death of his biological mother. As a consequence of this loss, she moved in with her aunt (sister of the deceased) and with her grandmother. Their living conditions were extremely poor, and he lived with many brothers and cousins, a result of the relationships that the aunt had had with various men. Sigfrido's father went home at night, drunk and looking for money. The child remembers himself at four years old, feeling terrified, hiding, waiting for his father who, if frustrated, could hit him savagely with his belt.

His oldest brother (five years older than Sigfrido) and Sigfrido himself decide to escape and walk to another city, far away, in search of some relatives who could help. Sigfrido remembers that his brother protected him from dangers on the streets and walking alone without any adult's support. He says that his brother was everything to him. When they arrived in this city, their relatives took them to a foster home run by some nuns, where Sigfrido lived until he was adopted.

Sigfrido retains the ability and cognitive-linguistic resources to express himself. He usually feels comfortable talking and tells the therapist that verbalising helps him a lot because he feels that it frees and unloads him emotionally.

Figure 6.2 A traumatic memory represented in Sigfrido's sandtray

Working on the integration of the traumatic contents (Block III) he began to tell me about his earliest memories. In his lifeline were abuse and abandonment from his father, and his mother's death. Sigfrido had previously worked on emotional regulation and empowerment, and he could associate his current symptoms of anger and aggressiveness with his harsh early life experiences. He got stuck while he was talking (See Figure 6.2).

SIGFRIDO: Words won't come out, I don't know how to express what happened and what I feel, I'm like... I don't know...

THERAPIST: Stuck?

SIGFRIDO: Yes.

THERAPIST: How do you feel about going to the shelf and do whatever you want about this early memory of your father's abuse and your mother's death? Let the miniatures choose you, let yourself go, don't think too much. Ok? Choose a figure that represents you.

SIGFRIDO: Yes, yes... I think it's a good idea.

And he created the scene that we can see above. He agreed to co-explore what he created in the tray. We asked him (slowly, allowing him to think quietly) the questions in table 1.1. He briefly explained that the little lion represented him. The big lion protecting him was his brother. The little lion must face all the dangers of life (symbolised in the miniatures from left to right: the soldier with the bow, the pirate with the pistol, the warrior with the sword, death and a skull warrior). Those characters want to hurt him, mistreat him and kill him. In the background to the left, there was a man who left and left the little lion alone. He feels hate towards him. Lying down is the mother of the little lion, dead. He feels sorry, very sorry for her.

THERAPIST: What does the little lion feel now?

SIGFRIDO: (Upset) Hate, a lot of hate...

THERAPIST: Where on the body does the lion feel that?

SIGFRIDO: In the chest.

THERAPIST: And what is he thinking?

SIGFRIDO: That they are going to hurt him and that he wants to hurt.

THERAPIST: How disturbing is the feeling of hatred in the chest that the lion is feeling now? Zero would be nothing and ten the highest you can imagine.

SIGFRIDO: Eight.

THERAPIST: Look at the scene and bring the whole experience (thought, emotion, sensation) to mind. When you have it, tell me.

SIGFRIDO: I have it.

(We apply bilateral stimulation according to the EMDR protocol -Eye Movement Desensitisation and Reprocessing[1]. It is a technique that allows to reprocess traumatic contents. Sigfrido had a good emotional connection with his body and was able to work according to this protocol.)

Later, when the level of disturbance reached zero, after several sets of bilateral stimulation, we asked if he wanted to modify the sandtray or leave it that way (see Figure 6.3)

Figure 6.3 Sigfrido wanted to change it and made the scene we see in this picture: he was able to reprocess this traumatic memory

The young man agreed, again, to co-explore the new sandtray. He claimed that the little lion had grown stronger. He thought he could fight. He felt that he could face danger. The man who left was no longer there, he belonged to the past. The little lion's mother was also left behind, but he felt that she was part of the lion's life and therefore placed her in the farthest corner, where past events are. He explained that the little lion will always keep a good memory of her. The big lion will always be there, he is sure of that, because he has helped and supported the little lion a lot (he got emotional and cried but did not lose control. We made a long silence). Thanks to him, he is alive. Sigfrido felt calmer and calmer after finishing this sandtray.

We were working with other sandtrayes in which he represented other traumatic contents of his life. At the end of therapy, the symptoms of aggressiveness towards his adoptive parents improved remarkably and he felt calmer, more stable on an emotional level and happier with his life. Two years later—trauma can resurface at other times in life—he returned to psychotherapy because he began a romantic relationship with a girl which triggered the fear of abandonment again.

Without the sandtray, Sigfrido would not have been able to tackle this arduous and difficult task. He had to represent those overwhelming contents of his mind, release emotions and process the event, giving it a new meaning: from the belief that "they are going to hurt me" to "I can fight", this change is a sign that the event were reprocessed. He began to perceive and value his life with the eyes of the present, without the need to feel aggressive, because he finally learned that no one was going to hurt him or abandon him. In this case, in addition to the co-exploration of the sandtray, we combined this technique with the EMDR approach, enhancing the positive results of the intervention. It is another example of directive methodology to deal with traumatic contents.

Creating life story narrative by reconstructing a coherent sense of *self*

Why are narratives important?

Many of the people (children or adults) who come to psychotherapy present the need to reconstruct their life history in order to develop a sense of *self* over time (self-awareness).

Before explaining how the sandtray can be a very helpful tool for this task (because the technique involves the use of symbols -miniatures- and a grammar -the created scene-), we must dedicate a few lines to the **importance of the narratives**, especially **for those whose life story is not integrated** as feel as if they were a broken mirror. Trauma has affected their brain/mind so much that they remember disjointed and disordered traces of their life (there are alterations in attention/memory); they do not know about the occurrence of certain events; they do not know how to locate the main events chronologically; they have developed their imagination to fill in the gaps and try to find some meaning; they idealise; there are events that they cannot remember because they happened in a stage prior to the three years of age.

Why are narratives important? Traumas involve disruptions in the flow of information that is physically based on the neural wiring (Siegel, 2007). Neural networks are patterns of neurochemical activation that carry information (of cognitive, sensory, emotional nature). If that flow is continuous and harmonic, it is because the environmental programming that orchestrates brain development was done in a balanced way: no serious life events produced that disturbance in the flow of communication. Metaphorically speaking, the brain is like a river that runs smoothly through the centre of its channel (Siegel, 2007; 2011).

But when serious, potentially traumatic, ongoing events occurred at an early age—and even later—this flow of information can be compromised. The person does not develop a sense of *self* over time. They may be aware of certain facts and events, but not fully aware of themselves; they may not feel themselves throughout their life in a coherent way. The person feels, as we mentioned earlier, like a broken, fragmented mirror. That is what trauma is: a defect in the integration of all the overloading experiences (cognitive, sensory, emotional...) of life that have not given rise to the construction of the person's *self* over time (Siegel, 2007).

To understand this better, let's think about ourselves for a moment: let's start to evoke and try to remember as early as we can. Let's remember the faces of our parents, where we played, ate, our first contacts, kisses, caresses... The first explicit memories. The first bonds of attachment and the people who have marked your lives.

The vast majority of us have lived and gone through adverse events; but there probably was someone with us who stayed and made us feel sense (Siegel, 2007). They made us feel safe and trusted.

In any case, many of us have not suffered from hunger, war, calamities, sexual abuse, physical and emotional abuse, or early loss of significant people... These terrible misfortunes have happened to many of the children, young and adults we work with: it is an immense pain that invades their body and mind from a very young age.

Therefore, we coherently remember that we went to such school in such year, our first trip or partner; our body/mind did not remove anything from consciousness because nothing was so shocking and threatening enough to cause that mechanism.

Our body, emotions, thoughts, sensations go together. We have an organised and coherent memory of everything we have experienced, but at the same time we have a regulated emotional memory of what happened (one memory goes hand in hand with the other). In short, we see ourselves over time (coherent sense of *self*) (Siegel, 2007).

Abandoned and abused children (and sometimes adults too) who are very likely to have suffered trauma cannot evoke memories without breaking down, without going through a high psychophysiological dysregulation. Sometimes they do not or cannot remember. Going back to the metaphor, we would say that they have the mirror, but it is broken, and the pieces need to be glued back together. And gluing it back together hurts a lot. Their life was loaded with multiple adversities/traumas that have undermined their security. In addition, they ended up learning various strategies in the past that, in their current life, turn out to be clearly counterproductive and even inadequate; but they were very useful in the past (they were their defences) and in many cases, it is thanks to them that they could survive.

Siegel (2007) states that narratives are very important for neurobiological development. As he states in his book *"The Developing Mind: "...narratives could originate as a fundamental part of social discourse. Stories try to make sense of events and the mental experiences of characters. Stories work to create a sense of coherent understanding of the individual in the world over time. The mind makes an integrative effort to create a sense of coherence in its own states across different times and contexts"*.

The minor will try to find meaning to what they have experienced, but it can be extremely incoherent, fragmented, loose, disjointed... That is where we observe that their brain/mind has not been integrated. They will need the help of an adult to reconstruct their story and rebuild themselves.

But exposing a patient to face-to-face verbal narration can be retraumatising, as well as inappropriate when working with minors. They need other means of expression, adapted—as we have mentioned throughout the book—to their possibilities and resources.

Using the sandtray technique, as we have explained in this work—with directive or non-directive methodology—is already a way of working on aspects of the patient's life, trying to integrate all modes of experience (sensory, emotional, intellectual).

But sometimes we need to work explicitly with the technique to reconstruct the patient's life story or of an important period of their life. **The sandtray is a tool that can be used to support narratives and reconstruct life story, making the experience cognitive but also sensory, emotional, kinesthetic.**

How to therapeutically work on life story using the sandtray

After several approaches based on non-directive methodology, there are adult and minor patients with psychological resources who agree to work on the reconstruction of their life story using the sandtray with a directive approach. It can be done with just one sandtray, or several may be needed to recreate different periods of life (or the same period).

Adult patient. We ask them to choose a miniature that represents them and make a scene about what happened to them at that moment or period of life.

Later, in the exploration phase, we suggest (because the person can handle themselves internally at a psychological level and has regulatory resources) that the patient verbally narrates what is happening in the tray, always referring to the miniature that represents them with the term they use. We must try to ensure that the patient does not make a literal or intellectual account that is disconnected from the emotion and body sensation – they may activate this type of thought. We must encourage them to pay attention and accept their emotions and body sensations, to try to feel them and manage them properly, without going outside the window of emotional tolerance, helping them in our role of therapists. We also make use of silences and phrases that reflect what the patient is saying.

In later sessions, with the photograph of the sandtray in front of us, we can rework on the story by writing it on a sheet of paper—even adding new aspects that may arise—and reading it while the patient looks at the sandtray. The therapist can read while the patient looks at the image of the sandtray and is connected to the emotion and body sensation.

Young patient. If they have enough psychological resources and is adequately supported and protected by at least one competent adult who meets their physical and emotional needs, an ideal developmental stage to undertake this task is around nine–ten years of age, pre-teenage. **The parents or adults responsible for the care of the minor can collaborate with the therapist in this task,** if they are competent, have fostered a secure bond with the child, are equipped with empathy and knowledge on how to calm and regulate the child or adolescent. The presence of the parents helps to share that peak moment of life, connect with the child or young person, show empathic receptivity and support them in this hard and painful process of reconstruction.

Parents or caregivers can make a sandtray with the child (this may not be necessary if the minor is a teenager): they should make a tray together about a period of life, or a specific moment, in which it is important to recreate the story and also provide a coherent and realistic narrative of hope (Cyrulnik et al., 2004).

We usually present this way of working with the sandtray to adopted and fostered minors and adults who need to rework on their harsh life stories, releasing emotions and developing **new meanings** about previous prolonged experiences of abuse or abandonment.

Let's see an example: the therapist proposes to the family and the minor that they make a sandtray about the day they went to look for them at the orphanage or nursery. The child or teenager must choose the miniature that represents him/her, and the parents select theirs. It is about them collaborating and following the child in this symbolic creation, setting reasonable limits, but taking into account that they should not direct the minor in what they want to do and choose. They should not teach, explain or indoctrinate him in any way, but rather they support them, guide them, connect with them emotionally, show empathy, share the experience, regulate them if needed, calm them down, make them feel safe (in the

Figure 6.4 The past and the present in Leopoldo's world in the sandtray

present moment and in that safe environment that is the therapy room) and, finally, help them structure and organise the scene in the tray by providing a coherent narrative.

By working with the sandtray in this way we are using a semi-directive methodology. It is a type of approach that moves away from the classic use of this therapeutic tool but which, in my experience, offers very good therapeutic results.

With certain parents or adults, previous therapy sessions with the child where they play together and they learn to tune in, support, emotionally reflect and follow the child's game within basic limits may be necessary.

We are going to see an example of how we work the narrative with a nine-year-old boy and his parents (adopted when he was two) using the sandtray. They recreated the scene of the day they adopted him, the most important day in the life of all minors and families, since it is when they begin to belong to it forever. With adopted minors, this is an ideal choice as it strengthens the bond and sharing the experience is emotionally gratifying for everyone. Later on, other moments or periods can be worked on, choosing from the most to the least disturbing.

The minor must have enough regulatory resources (they had to learn them in Block I) and that the parents or caregivers can contain and regulate the child[2], that they know how to comfort and calm him/her and that the minor takes advantage comfort to calm down and, when they are back within the window of emotional tolerance, go back to the narrative.

As we can see in Figure 6.4, in the background on the left, we can see the parents just before taking the plane to go to Leopoldo's country of origin. Fences separate past from present. The stewardess is waiting for them to board the plane and travel. On the side that represents his country and the orphanage, there is the doctor (he was not there that day, but Leopoldo wanted to introduce this symbol of healing and care), a caregiver and the children (including the one representing him). They are in the garden. The house where they lived is located to the right of the photograph. They were changing the scene while narrating.

The names of the people as well as places and circumstances have been changed for anonymity.

The narrative: How Leopoldo's parents went looking for him at the orphanage and the thread that unites them was tied forever between them

THERAPIST: Leopoldo, stand between your parents and if you want you can hold their hand at any time.

(Leopoldo and his parents move the miniatures and dramatise, telling the story as narrators but also making the characters speak. The therapist intervenes to reflect, ask or add important elements to the narrative)

THE FATHER: We're going to go to Chile for Leopoldo! We got on the plane!
THERAPIST: How do the parents feel?

THE MOTHER: I'm super nervous but happy at the same time.

THE FATHER: Nervous and happy at the same time.

THE MOTHER: She is so pretty, she looks so happy, she's going to meet her son!

THERAPIST: Is this the most important day of your life?

PARENTS: (*at once*) The best day, without a doubt!

THE MOTHER: (*joking*) Well, the day on the plane isn't really the best, no. The best day is when we kiss and hug our child tight.

THE FATHER: They are a little nervous and scared because everything is unknown to them, but they're very eager to meet their son.

(The figures approach the fence)

THE FATHER: They really want to meet Leopoldo...

THERAPIST: Who receives them?

THE FATHER: Well, the director of the orphanage and the educator.

THE MOTHER: Hello, we've come to meet Leopoldo! Can we come in?

THERAPIST: I wonder how the child is feeling right now...

LEOPOLDO: Well...

THERAPIST: Do you feel sad, alone...?

(Pauses)

LEOPOLDO: He feels sad. Yes.

THERAPIST: It's normal for you to feel this way. Do you feel it now?

LEOPOLDO: Yes.

THERAPIST: It's okay to feel sad. Let yourself feel it. Do the parents feel that he had to go through an orphanage, feeling sad?

THE MOTHER: Of course! It's painful. Because although he was with children and caregivers, he didn't have any parents. They were missing.

LEOPOLDO: Yes. Go on.

THE EDUCATOR: I'm going to take you to meet Leopoldo who is sick today, he's got chickenpox and a fever. Well, maybe it'd be better to see him another day...

PARENTS: We don't care, we came looking for him, we want to see him (*with emotional emphasis*). We really want to see him, we've been waiting a long time. We're not leaving here until we meet him.

FATHER: Let's go where he is!

(The mother now acts as the narrator, speaking and moving the miniatures of the parents, who reach the room where Leopoldo was, very excited)

THE NURSE: Leopoldo is the one is playing with the bear.

THE MOTHER: And you looked at us and...

THE FATHER: You started crying...

MOTHER: Of course, you did, you were surprised. Then, your father gave you a piggyback...

THE FATHER: (*while rocking the miniature baby*): Oh my dear child! (*in a loving tone*) It's so beautiful! And we started crying...

(Silence)

THE MOTHER: ...Out of joy, huh!

THERAPIST: I wonder how the child is feeling now.

THE FATHER: Give me a big, big hug... (*the miniatures talking to each other*)

LEOPOLDO: (*softly and calmly*) Good.

THERAPIST: How's the child feeling?

LEOPOLDO: Cheerful.

THE MOTHER: I took him, and he started crying with me. But that wasn't your fault, Leopoldo. When mothers are a little nervous, children can feel it and start crying too. You didn't know me either. And you were even sick! The poor thing had a high temperature... But then we started playing and he felt better. With the bear and a stroller...

THE FATHER: And he started smiling and... Everything was great! Everyone was super happy!

THE MOTHER: Yes!

(Leopoldo smiles and hugs his parents for a while. They kiss him lovingly. They stay like that for a while)

THERAPIST: This is a great moment. The most important of your lives. It happened seven years ago, in 2006. That day is the day you became part of this family forever. You will never be separated again. No matter what.

PARENTS: Of course!

THE MOTHER: That day, since he was sick, they didn't let us go out. And we had to be with him inside playing...

THERAPIST: Too bad he was sick just that day!

THE FATHER: But he recovered soon!

THE MOTHER: We brought him lunch and snacks every day until he felt better.

THE FATHER: He ate everything... Juices, baby food... Everything!

THERAPIST: I can imagine that the parents were impatient to go back home with Leopoldo.

PARENTS: Yes!

THE MOTHER: We were waiting for the papers he needed to leave his home country. We had to be given authorisation.

THE FATHER: Until the papers finally arrived. Because you are our son, you already were, but you needed those paper to leave the country!

THE FATHER: Look, Leopoldo, we can go now, I've got the papers!

THE MOTHER: We were really happy that day...

THERAPIST: I wonder if the boy wants to say goodbye to the place where he was born.

THE FATHER: We said goodbye to everyone and left.

THE MOTHER: Bye!

LEOPOLDO: Goodbye, goodbye...!

THERAPIST: It's an orphanage that your birth mother took you to, she was very young, almost a child, and couldn't take care of you. The people in that place took care of you the best they could. They gave you what you needed. But the best place to live is a family.

LEOPOLDO: Yes! (happy)

THE FATHER: Well, bye! Hold my hand while we're leaving.

THE MOTHER: We went out the door, got in a car and then on the plane. You'd never taken a plane before! You liked it so much, so much that you fell asleep...

(The boy takes his miniature back to the orphanage, and again takes it to his parents)

THE MOTHER: We can go see your country whenever you want. We love the place where you were born and the mother who gave you life.

THERAPIST: Yes, Leopoldo is like a tree with two roots: one belongs to the land where he was born and where his birth mother couldn't take care of him. And another root is the one that belongs to his foster family and the land that will see him grow up and become older, having a family that gives him everything he needs to feel good, safe and protected.

(Leopoldo nods his head)

THE MOTHER: At first you were nervous, but then you calmed down. We were super comfortable. And at home... We gave you a pacifier for the first time.

THERAPIST: And now you'll be with this family forever and ever. Do you remember the game of the magic rope of love? It was created here, forever. How are you feeling now?

LEOPOLDO: Very good!

THE FATHER: When we got home, the whole family came looking for us and welcomed you, with the dog too. What a beautiful boy! Everyone was kissing you.

THERAPIST: And so began Leopoldo's new life, from the day he went to his foster family for the first time. The one that will take care of him and love him. They will always be happy together, no matter what happens. Even if they fight and argue… He will never go back to an orphanage and they will never leave him alone and sad.

Notes

1 To learn more about the EMDR approach, look up the website of the EMDR Spain Association: emdr-es.org
2 An essential requirement to be able to benefit from this kind of task is that the life context of the minor is stable, rich in affection and boundaries, with at least one responsible caregiver. If not, this therapeutic intervention should not be done. If life context is changing, it does not protect and does not satisfy the basic physical and psychological needs of the minor, it is useless to work in therapy. It can even be counterproductive.

References

Barudy, J. (1998). *El dolor invisible de la infancia. Una lectura ecosistémica del maltrato infantil*. Barcelona: Paidós Ibérica.

Barudy, J. & Dantagnan, M. (2005). *Los buenos tratos a la infancia. Parentalidad, apego y resiliencia*. Barcelona: Gedisa.

Barudy, J. & Dantagnan, M. (2010). *Los desafíos invisibles de ser madre o padre. Manual de evaluación de las competencias y la resiliencia parental*. Barcelona: Gedisa.

Barudy, J. & Dantagnan, M. (2012). *La fiesta mágica y realista de la resiliencia infantil: Manual y técnicas terapéuticas para apoyar y promover la resiliencia de los niños, niñas y adolescentes*. Barcelona: Gedisa.

Barudy, J. & Dantagnan, M. (2014). *La trauma-terapia sistémica aplicada a los niños, niñas y adolescentes afectados por traumas. Un modelo basado en los buenos tratos y la promoción de la resiliencia*. Powerpoint presentado en el marco del Diplomado en trauma terapia infantil sistémica. Bilbao: Documento no publicado.

Benito, R. (2015). *Neurobiología del trauma*. Powerpoint preentado en el Postgrado en traumaterapia infantil sistémica de Barudy y Dantagnan. San Sebastián: Documento no publicado.

Benito, R. (2020). *La regulación emocional. Bases neurobiológicas y desarrollo en la infancia y adolescencia*. Madrid: El Hilo Ediciones.

Cyrulnik, B. (2003). *El murmullo de los fantasmas*. Barcelona: Gedisa.

Cyrulnik, B., Vanistendael, S., Guénard, T. et al. (2004). *El realismo de la esperanza. Testimonios de experiencias profesionales en torno a la resiliencia*. Barcelona: Gedisa Editorial.

Cyrulnik, B. (2015). *Las almas heridas*. Barcelona: Gedisa.

Cyrulnik, B. (2020). *Escribí soles de noche. Literatura y resiliencia*. Barcelona: Gedisa.

Dantagnan, M (2015). *La caja de arena, el trauma y la resiliencia*. Powerpoint presentado en el Postgrado en traumaterapia infantil sistémica de Barudy y Dantagnan. Barcelona: Documento no publicado.

Gómez, A.M. (2013). *EMDR and adjunct approaches with children. Complex trauma, attachment and dissociation*. New York: Springer Publishing Company.

González, A. & Mosquera, D. (2012). *EMDR y disociación. El abordaje progresivo.* Madrid: Ediciones Pleyades.

Ogden, P. & Fisher, J. (2016). *Psicoterapia sensoriomotriz. Intervenciones para el trauma y el apego.* Bilbao: Desclée de Brouwer.

Porges, S.W. (2011). *The polyvagal theory: neurophysiological foundations of emotions, attachment, communication and self-regulation.* New York: W.W. Norton & Company.

Puig, G. & Rubio, J.L. (2011). *Manual de resiliencia aplicada.* Barcelona: Gedisa.

Schore, A. (2003). *Affect Dysregulation and disorders of the self.* W.W. Norton & Company: London.

Siegel, D.J. (2007). *La mente en desarrollo. Cómo interactúan las relaciones y el cerebro para modelar nuestro ser.* Bilbao: Desclée de Brouwer.

Siegel, D.J. (2011). *Mindsight: La nueva ciencia de la transformación personal.* Barcelona: Paidós Ibérica.

Steele, K., Nijenhuis, E. & Van der Hart, O. (2008). *El yo atormentado: la disociación estructural y el tratamiento de la traumatización crónica.* Bilbao: Desclée de Brouwer.

Wallin, D. (2012). *El apego en psicoterapia.* Bilbao: Desclée de Brouwer.

Chapter 7

Neurobiology of the Sandtray Technique

Introduction

The baby is born with a nervous system to make; with a basic neural device whose purpose is to bond with the adult responsible for them, and to take advantage of the interaction with the adult to shape its functioning in a vertically and horizontally integrated way (Siegel, 2007). When it comes to the nervous system, integrated functioning occurs when its various components operate harmoniously in order to maximise the chances of survival and enjoyment; an activity in which they all have something to say, and no nucleus or area suffocates the activity of the others, they do not rule over the others or dominate longer than it is needed to serve the objectives of the individual. Vertical integration includes the relationship between the brain and the body, plus the relationship between the prefrontal cortex and the limbic system; horizontal integration occurs when both cerebral hemispheres co-operate.

Traumatic experiences are a threat to that integration; especially those that occur within an interpersonal relationship, as is the case with experiences of child abuse in any of its forms: physical, emotional, sexual or neglect and abandonment. Neurodevelopment during the first years of life organises the nervous system thanks to the interaction with attachment figures; and research shows that, if interactions of abandonment or abuse occur in that very special bond, the areas of the nervous system will develop in a way that makes it difficult to achieve that integrated functioning (Teicher, Samson, Anderson & Ohashi, 2016).

The lack of vertical integration will affect the emotional regulation device, predisposing to states in which passions control behaviour, giving rise to an emotional hijacking of brain functions; it will also affect the relationship between the nervous system and the body, producing disorders of the neuro-endocrine-immune system that can end up causing problems as harmful as hypertension or obesity. But vertical integration is not the only one that suffers because of early trauma; the horizontal integration that emerges from the interaction between the two cerebral hemispheres is also impaired. Therefore, children who have experienced early trauma may find it difficult to

DOI: 10.4324/9781003359111-7

symbolise, will more often suffer from alexithymia, an inability to name and describe affective states, and will typically lack a narrative of the traumatic experience, so they will preferentially resort to behaviour to express what they feel.

Some of the most effective forms of traumatic damage treatment consists of restoring integrated functioning in the nervous system. This is the case, for example, of eye movement desensitisation and reprocessing (EMDR) therapies, which facilitate a reprocessing of the traumatic experience by involving the whole brain (Boukezzi et al., 2017) (Chen, Zhang, Hu & Liang, 2015) (Landin-Romero, Moreno-Alcazar, Pagani & Amann, 2018). What I intend to show in this chapter is that the sandtray is an ideal technique for the same purpose, and it also has some advantages over other forms of diagnosis and treatment. As we will see, its playful nature is a source of implicit and spontaneous emotional regulation that facilitates work with people damaged by trauma almost from the first session. While making a tray, the patient also enters a state of therapeutic dissociation. The traumatic contents are going to take shape in the world of the tray without being detected, without exciting the defensive operations of the nervous system that often lead to emotional lack of control or avoidance; and it is beneficial because the world in the tray is often a reflection of ineffable and threatening experiences, which returns to the nervous system that created it and reintegrates as a narrative during the co-exploration phase of the world in the sand.

In the waiting room: remembering trauma

An 11-year-old boy sits in the waiting room waiting for his therapist. He was told it will help him get over the pain and the sadness caused by all the "bad things" his father did when he would go to his room to kiss him goodnight. Since when this happened, he cannot help but feel an anger inside, pushing him to hit and break things; that is why he was expelled from school. He does not enjoy doing it, but he cannot control it. Although he has been told that the person he is going to see can help him, the boy is nervous. Surely this person will ask him again about the places where his father touched him, how long that contact lasted and how it ended. As he thinks about it, he cannot help but feel fear and disgust again; he imagines himself talking about it as he did to that doctor in the hospital, so stuck-up and cold, as if he was doing a history exam at school. The memories make him shiver slightly, feel some kind of weakness in his legs and a knot in his stomach. He wonders if the person who is going to see him now will be like that doctor, or rather kind and loving.

The child is about to face a new experience and his brain is preparing to deal with it. That is why his memory is recovering similar experiences. If we could see the state of his brain, we would discover that when he tries to predict the future, he activates the same areas of the nervous system corresponding to the memory of events already experienced (Szpunar, Watson & McDermott, 2007). Therefore, while waiting for the therapist, he evokes previously known similar figures, with whom he faced similar tasks, thus anticipating possible outcomes. He anticipates the future by remembering the past.

Every time we experience a situation, the neural connection networks that make up the nervous system are activated, producing an electrochemical representation of what is being experienced. Colours and shapes activate the neural networks of the visual cortex, and sounds do the same in the auditory cortex. Different visual or sound experiences will produce different activation states in the networks that process these sensations, in such a way that the conformation of this active network is different depending on the environmental experience that produces it.

Memory depends on the ability to repeat activation patterns of neuronal groups. Therefore, remembering is reproducing the brain activity generated by what is remembered. The probability that the same neural network that responded to a given stimulus will be activated again depends on the number of times it has done so, the number of times it has been activated. Hence, one of the bases of learning is repetition, although not necessarily repetition in the presence of the stimulus. Reactivating these networks when something is evoked helps to consolidate them; as it happens when a student mentally repeats the lesson. Therefore, remembering is also reconsolidating the contents of memory, to the extent that it facilitates the creation and reactivation of networks. The other component that facilitates the consolidation of these networks is the emotional state experienced during the experience of the stimulus; if the emotion is intense enough, it can produce rapid learning, reducing the number of repetitions needed to consolidate memory. This is one of the reasons why traumatic experiences often leave such persistent memories.

Remembering does not mean looking for a folder with documents in an archive; it rather consists of re-reproducing the cerebral state that took place when what is wanted to be evoked was learned; restoring, as far as possible, the same state of neuronal activity. In the act of remembering something, all the brain areas that were activated when learning occurred are involved. Neural networks located in different areas of the brain allow us to access various aspects of memory, depending on the type of stimulus they are responsible for processing. Those that deal with sensory stimuli help us remember images, sounds or other sensations. In the case of our child, the memory of the doctor evokes "the vision of a very serious man in a white room that smelled of alcohol". Recovering these sensations requires activating the cortical areas related to the corresponding sensation: the visual cortex (located in the posterior, occipital pole of the brain), the auditory cortex (in the temporal lobe) and the olfactory cortex (in the anterior and internal area of the temporal lobe) are activated by repeating the same state with which they were turned on when that situation was experienced.

The memory of sensory experiences feeds an aspect of memory called *perceptual* ("what a father looks like" "what a doctor looks like"). Little by little, the repetition of experiences related to these images give meaning to what is perceived. Repeated contact with people who say they want to heal or help will make the words "doctor", "nurse" or "therapist", and the visual sensations associated with these figures, evoke a predictable sequence of events. *Semantic* memory retains the meaning of words, objects and concepts: "what a father is and how he is expected to behave with a child", "what a doctor is and what I can expect from my relationship with him". It mostly depends on the activity of an area in the temporal lobe called Wernicke's area, which retains meanings related to language and social interactions (Wang et al., 2015). Throughout life, repeating experiences will create the *episodic* memory that allows access to data associated with the experiences of the individual in certain places and times ("at what time, how long and how often my father did bad things to me when he came to say good night"; "How long ago I was in the hospital talking to that doctor; what happened before and what happened after"). For its construction, the neural networks located in the parietal cortex are very important.

In learning, perceptual, semantic, and episodic memories function in a sequence. Tulving's model (Tulving, 2001; 2002) assumes that we initially learn through perceptual memory ("this is what a doctor looks like"); the repetition of certain perceptions generates semantic learning ("what a doctor is and what they are expected to do is"); finally, episodic memory is built to the extent that certain perceptions with a specific meaning are repeated ("what experiences I have had with doctors"). When all this learning is assembled, it becomes difficult to activate one of the forms of memory without dragging the corresponding contents of the other two. Thus, seeing someone who looks like a father (perceptive memory), reactivates the neural networks that bring the qualities associated with that figure (semantic memory) and the moments lived with him (episodic memory).

So far, we have dealt with **explicit memory** (Schacter & Wagner, 2013): it is responsible for storing data and facts that we can retrieve consciously and deliberately to build the story of what happened. Memories stored in explicit memory are created through collaboration between the prefrontal cortex (PFC, to be discussed later) and the **hippocampus** (Figure 7.3), a structure that looks like a seahorse (hence its name), buried in the temporal lobe.

The hippocampus functions as a kind of "search engine" or "librarian". It is not where memories are stored, but rather a device that encodes and files them in various places in the brain, and then knows where to find them and how to retrieve them. It evokes the contents of explicit memory in the same way that Google searches the Internet for requested information. When a memory is requested, the hippocampus activates the neural networks that reproduce the brain state that produced the stimulus or event to be remembered. Retrieval of learning also involves co-operation between the PFC and the hippocampus.

An important aspect of evocation is that it is not perfect. Remembering does not mean extracting a file from a folder; it is more like putting together a puzzle that is usually missing a piece. Our brain solves this problem by *reconstructing* what was remembered; it picks the essential, the most important or the most striking part, and fills in the gaps to make sense of the story. The patches added to complete the memory are not exactly chosen randomly: the current emotional state paints the memory in its colour, suppressing or adding data according to the attachment of the moment; memory can also be distorted by the effect of suggestion, when social pressure or indications from an influential person introduce false data (Schacter & Wagner, 2013).

Going back to Tulving's model, the formation of memories, learning, also goes in the opposite direction, from the episodic to the semantic. The repetition of certain episodes (such as encountering people who try to help) modifies the meaning (the semantic memory) of what is perceived—the experiences and the stimuli. For example, although a negative experience with a therapist has associated unpleasant content with that type of person, new experiences can correct the impression, adding more positive assessments to the situation and to the figure of "person who helps you when you are sick". However, it can also get worse: recovering negative memories consolidates these neural networks, carriers of terrifying content, making it increasingly likely that they will automatically reactivate in similar situations.

When meeting the therapist, the child recovers the data that he has stored in explicit memory, related to colours, shapes, sounds, places and things that he was told and spoke. But what about the shivers and "knot in the stomach" feeling that seem to be associated in the child's mind with the memory of the doctor and what his father did to him? Are those internal bodily sensations part of your memory? As a matter of fact, they are. Our processing systems constantly receive information from the outside world; moreover—and very often we are not even aware of this—they manage data related to our internal organs, and this data can also be consolidated in the form of brain activation patterns, associated or not with those that come from our senses (Damasio, 2020). That is why our child cannot help but feel a bad stomach, the palms of his hands slightly sweating and occasional jumps in his chest when he remembers the doctor and his father; the episodic and semantic memories associated with these two figures are stimulated by the changes they produced in the body.

This neuronal activity corresponds to a special type of memory called **implicit memory** (Kandel et al., 2000). It also depends on the ability of neurons to activate "here and now" in the same way that they did "there and before." Just as explicit memory depends on a complex apparatus of interactions between various brain regions, implicit memory only needs a network of connected neurons. That is why it exists since when the first neuronal connections developed (synapses), towards the sixth or seventh week of intrauterine life, and it will stay with us for the rest of life.

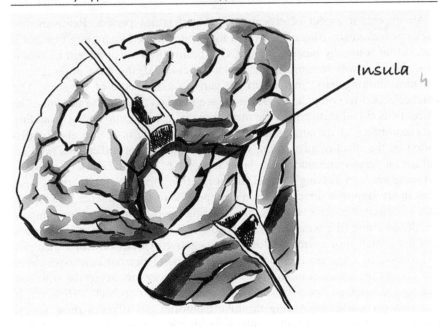

Figure 7.1 The insula is a key area for the perception of internal states

There are some differences in the features of these two types of memory. The contents of explicit memory can be counted; we can consciously operate with them by establishing new associations. That is why it is a richer and more flexible type of memory. In contrast, the memories stored in implicit memory are patterns of brain activation related to physiological states or dispositions for action; they have much to do with emotional states, they cannot be put into words, and they are not as modifiable as those contained in explicit memory. Implicit learning does not require the participation of the hippocampus or the prefrontal cortex; the persistent and repeated activation of neural networks in areas such as the limbic system and the insula a remote region of the cerebral cortex related to the processing of emotions and body states, is enough. Because evoking explicit content involves a reproduction of brain states generated by past stimuli, it somewhat implies time travel; but the episodic form of this memory can place the memories in time, causing us to retain the sensation of remembering, not reliving. In contrast, implicit memory does not mark any information about time; there is no way to temporarily place the evocations corresponding to the implicit memories, so their activity is often a way of reliving the past.

For the victim of trauma, remembering and relating the abuse suffered involves recovering explicit and implicit brain states that bring the nervous system back to the same state of activation that it experienced during the traumatic event; moreover, as with any type of learning, the repetition of these states over and over again can consolidate the pain and the traumatic experience. That is why the situation in which victims of trauma evoke the pain experienced is so important: if they remember the trauma in a cold or hostile context (as often happens before legal or medical officials who are not very sensitive to trauma), or do so when they do not have the necessary resources to regulate their emotions yet, they will reproduce (and reconsolidate) the neural states that occurred during the traumatic damage. This will increase the likelihood that they will suffer the symptoms of re-experiencing the trauma, typical of a post-traumatic stress disorder, throughout their evolution. Much of the effect of the therapeutic intervention must be to reactivate neural networks, but to do so in a situation that introduces changes in them that rebuild and reconsolidate in a restorative way; modifying the implicit contents and reformulating the explicit ones to integrate both in a way that mitigates the pain.

Explicit memory works with data coming mainly from sensors that detect changes in the external environment, especially sight and hearing. The information constituting the implicit memory comes from sensors aimed at monitoring changes inside of us. Examples are the state of our stomach, the tension of joint ligaments, the level of muscle relaxation or contraction and hoe much our lungs are filling up or emptying. The relationship between this

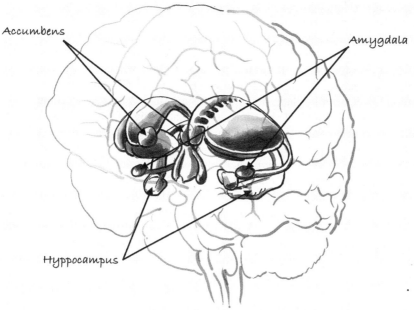

Figure 7.2 The amygdala, accumbens and hippocampus are critical components of the limbic system

nervous activity and emotional states—which, to begin with, are nothing more than states of physiological activation (Damasio, 2011)—is evident. All this information is constantly transmitted through the autonomic nervous system and the peripheral nervous system to a) the areas of the cerebral cortex involved in somatosensory processing, in the case of muscles and ligaments; and b) in the case of the visceral state, especially to the **insula** (see Figure 7.1). This area of the cerebral cortex, hidden behind the Silvyan Fissure, seems to be the crossroads where neuroceptive information ("how I am") is combined with data related to the external world ("what is happening around me").

The sum of all the information generated by these receptors constitutes a kind of "sixth sense" called **neuroception** (Porges, 2009). Neuroception is an important source of emotional and social cognition. The brain cannot think about emotions without physically reconstructing or simulating them (Niedenthal, Winkielman, Mondillon & Vermeulen, 2009). Hence, to describe emotional states we use terms related to physical sensations ("I feel a knot in my stomach", "I'm about to explode", "don't get me mad"). This physical simulation based on the perception of muscle contraction states also facilitates the detection of other people's emotional states: we find it more difficult to recognise the emotion associated with facial expressions when the muscles of our own face do not contract to make us feel what we see in the face of our interlocutor (Hennenlotter et al., 2009) (Havas, Glenberg, Gutowski, Lucarelli & Davidson, 2010).

Neuroception is also at the base of intuition, the hunch that makes us sense things. Unconscious somatic signals from the Autonomic Nervous System tell us which decision is correct, even if we do not know what rules are helping us to decide (Bechara, Damasio, Tranel & Damasio, 1997), which makes neuroception a source of implicit, non-conscious and non-deliberate learning.

One form of implicit learning is conditioning. Conditioned learning requires temporary association of two events (needle/syringe and pain). When both are associated in a regular way, the appearance of one activates the brain pattern corresponding to the implicit memory of the other. In this way, in the classic Pavlov experiment, the dog implicitly "evoked" the activation of the neurons that produced salivary secretion at the possibility of eating steak when it heard a bell. One of the most important brain nuclei for conditioned learning is the **amygdala** (see Figure 7.2) (Ferry, Wirth & Di Scala, 1999; Killcross, Robbins & Everitt, 1997). Buried in the basal zone of the brain, it is fundamentally responsible for learning which stimuli are related to a threat and triggering defensive reactions and responses to stress through the hypothalamus and the autonomic nervous system. Our amygdala responds to presumably threatening stimuli before the visual cortex has been able to identify the scene. In addition, fearful facial expressions activate it more than other scenes of danger (Méndez-Bértolo et al., 2016).

Neuroception is the soundtrack of our experiences, the emotional music that serves as the background to all experiences. It accompanies us constantly, it is inevitable, we cannot control it; despite not always being conscious, it will exert its influence without us realising it, guiding our perception and our behaviour. For example, in prosopagnosia (loss of the ability to recognise faces) the Autonomic Nervous System reacts to familiar faces, even though the individual is unable to recognise them (Bechara et al., 1997); in the same way, the hypothalamus and the tonsils activate in individuals who have lost detailed vision when shown scenes provoking anxiety (Denburg, Jones & Tranel, 2009).

Let's see how all this is working in our child. He is somewhat scared. He is preparing for the meeting with the therapist by using the PFC and the hippocampus to retrieve the only explicit memory associated with a helping relationship: that cold doctor who questioned him in that messy office. Along with these explicit memories the amygdala has inevitably activated neural networks associated with implicit content that evoke the anxiety linked to the events that it will predictably have to recount. The feeling of "knot in the stomach", the palpitations and the sweating of the palms indicate that the body is preparing to face a scary situation, and it does so through the activity of the autonomic nervous system.

The autonomic or vegetative section of our nervous system (**Autonomic Nervous System**, ANS) is responsible for collecting information from visceral sensors to transmit it to the central nervous system and bringing its response back to systems that function unconsciously, such as the cardiovascular system, the digestive system, the endocrine system and even the immune system. One of its most important tasks has to do with responding to threats. The ANS fulfils this function through two antagonistic sections. On the one hand, the parasympathetic through the vagus nerve that leaves the skull from nuclei located in the brain stem; and on the other the sympathetic mode through a chain of nerve roots that start from the spinal cord along its entire length.

The **parasympathetic system** triggers a response of immobility, reduction of metabolic rate and slowing of visceral functions. Its activation produces the "corpse reflex", a defensive response that we see in many mammals when faced with an inescapable threat and that causes fainting in humans, associated with emotionally intense situations. This reaction of immobilisation and disconnection depends on the dorsal nucleus of the vagus nerve and is produced in the form of *"I don't hate anything"*. The **sympathetic system**, for its part, produces a "storm of movement" or "fight/flight" response that leads to an acceleration of motor and visceral activity and an increase in energy expenditure.

If there were no mediator between the two, the perception of a threat would make us swing between fainting and uncontrollable anxiety. Fortunately, the human species has a modulatory system (Porges, 2017) which attenuates sympathetic activation without allowing it to drop to syncope.

This modulator is part of the parasympathetic system, but it depends on one of the nuclei of the **vagus nerve**, located in the brainstem and emitting fast-transmission myelinated fibres that respond quickly to orders from the central nervous system, producing a state of "safe stillness" or "attentive calm". Its activity allows to maintain the state of low metabolic output and psychomotor inhibition typical of the parasympathetic system, without reducing the beneficial state of alertness generated by the sympathetic system.

While waiting for the therapist, the implicit and explicit evocations provoke in the child an increased activity of the sympathetic system; at the same time, the ventral branch of the vagus tries to modulate this activation by reducing the instinctive tendency to escape and preventing an involuntary response of disconnection from the environment in the form of a cadaveric reflex or vasovagal syncope.

First meeting with the therapist: perception corrects memory

*Suddenly, the door to the therapy room opens, **the room of the brave**, and the therapist comes out with another child. The activation of the sympathetic nervous system and increased levels of norepinephrine have made the boy's senses more receptive; the sound of the door, along with this increased alertness, startle him. He sees another child about his age walk past him; on his shoulder, the hand of a somewhat thick man rests gently, and he smiles as he says goodbye to the little patient with a sweet, loving tone. The memory of the doctor has*

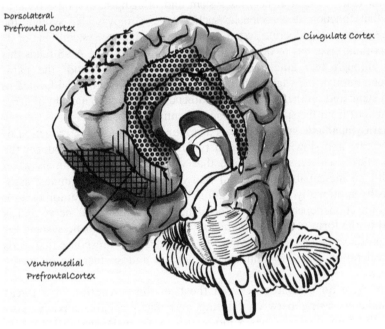

Figure 7.3 The cingulate cortex is involved in assessing the risks and benefits of behaviour.

caused a change in the sensitivity and focus of the child's sensory receptors. His sight and hearing, following the orders of the brain, interested above all in discovering similarities or differences between the current experience and the previous one, try to clearly identify the physiognomy, facial expression and tone of voice of the psychologist to confirm or rule out whether he resembles the doctor, whether he can expect different treatment from him.

Feeling and perceiving are different abilities. The sensation is the brain activation produced by the mere reaction of the sensors. The perception is the result of processing sensations to convert them into useful information, which gives meaning to experience and helps guide behaviour towards a good outcome. In the same way that remembering is not reproducing, but reconstructing, perceiving is not simply feeling, but organising sensations so that they acquire meaning.

Therefore, our perception is a combination of (Eagleman, 2013):
What our senses are capable of detecting. Our ears or our eyes are only sensitive to a limited range of frequencies of light or sound waves. In addition, they get bored easily and attenuate the response when the stimulation takes an invariable time, so that they can stop reacting, even if the stimulus persists. Sometimes the limitation is intentional; for example, our eyes move to selectively focus on what we find interesting or worrying; also ears, through the activity of the stapedius muscle, tense or relax the eardrum to select certain sound frequencies (Moore, Dalley & Agur, 2013). Porges has pointed out the importance of this muscular activity to select the sound frequencies that correspond to the maternal voice during the establishment of the attachment relationship (Porges, 2009).

How the processing centers interpret the sensations received. It seems to us that a smaller object is further away, and two lines that come together give us a sensation of depth. Other interpretations are based on previous experience, on memory, such as those we make about the meaning of the facial expressions and gestures of our fellow human beings. Finally, part of the processing will depend on the current neuroceptive state, which will act as an instruction that directs the sense organs so that they selectively attend to those stimuli that will confirm or not whether the fear is justified.

How the processing centres fill in the blanks, so that everything makes sense and an efficient response can be developed based on expectations. For example, although we perceive the image much earlier than the sound, the brain "edits" the sensations so that the sight of a clap is synchronized with the noise it produces. (Eagleman & Holcombe, 2002).

This work that transforms mere sensations into perceptions, giving them meaning and turning them into something manageable and known, is highly influenced by the neuroceptive state of the individual and by their explicit and implicit memory. Memory and neuroception generate a forecast of possible events in the brain. On the one hand, the amygdala preserves the memory of sensations that were once associated with danger or harm. If there is a threatening situation, an overactive amygdala or excessive implicit evocation could trigger an automatic fight or flight reaction which would leave no time to weigh possible courses of action. Whereas, if activation of the amygdala is moderate, certain brain areas that allow considering various options can intervene. One of these is the **cingulate cortex** (see Figure 7.3), located in the cerebral cortex, just above the corpus callosum. It is a kind of intelligence sensitive to experiences of pain and social rejection (Eisenberger, Lieberman & Williams, 2003). Attentive to the most relevant and emotionally significant stimuli (Weissman, Gopalakrishnan, Hazlett & Woldorff, 2005), it monitors and evaluates the result of actions (Botvinick, Cohen & Carter, 2004), detecting errors (Gehring & Fencsik, 2001) and reporting on the possible harms and benefits of each course of action (Bush, Luu, Posner & Posner, 2000). This report will be presented to the **prefrontal cortex** (see Figure 7.3; 7.4), the executive director, which is responsible for triggering a more or less elaborate behaviour whose purpose will be the achievement of the most profitable objective.

Before and during the task, the prefrontal cortex constantly refines the sensitivity of the sensory and interoceptive receptors, focusing above all on the data that best informs about the result of the forecasts and the smooth running of the process. It will do this by controlling, above all, a nucleus for the passage of sensory information, located at the base of the brain: the thalamus. This nucleus behaves like an equaliser that filters, suppresses or increases certain flows of sensory information to perceive what is most interesting. At the same time, it continues to study the reports from the cingulate, trying to contain the urgent stimulation of the amygdala that is drawing attention to the emotional sense of what is perceived, demanding a response in accordance with the needs demanded by the situation. Each new examination can confirm or rule out the prediction by emphasising the emergence of explicit and implicit memories that match or differ from it. If they match, the behaviour will be the same. If they are different, it will be necessary to modify the behaviour, correct the focus of the sensors and extract more memory material that provides clues to make a new prediction and resume the cycle.

As we have seen, the child is anxious. His prefrontal cortex is trying to keep the amygdala under control, so it doesn't trigger a panic response, it is using ventral vagus activation to keep the child from running away or shutting down, and it is regulating the flow of data in the thalamus to clearly analyse the therapist. "Should I fear him, or can I trust him?" At the same time, his hippocampus continues to recover the activity of neural networks that were activated during previous contact with adults who helped him on other occasions. Recovering these explicit memory networks inevitably activates implicit networks that intensify or not the current neuroception; in this way, the child will finally see if what he is experiencing now is similar or different to what he experienced then.

People who experienced abuse during childhood suffered neurodevelopmental disorders that generated a nervous system predisposed to non-integrated functioning; with an overactive amygdala (Tottenham et al., 2011) (Malter Cohen et al., 2013), an underdeveloped cingulate cortex (O'Doherty, Chitty, Saddiqui, Bennett & Lagopoulos, 2015); an incompetent prefrontal cortex (Herrera Ortiz, Rincón Cuenca & Fernández Beaujon, 2021; Teicher & Samson, 2016); and to top it off, a weak ventral vagal system, unable to mediate between the sympathetic and parasympathetic systems (Dale et al., 2009)(Green et al., 2016; McLaughlin, Rith-Najarian, Dirks & Sheridan, 2015). If the therapist does not take this into account, it is easy for the child to enter a state of emotional dysregulation during the session that will prevent the establishment of a positive bond and disrupt the course of the session. When the functioning of the nervous system disintegrates, an overactive amygdala can seize power and easily cause the resignation of an incompetent prefrontal and cingulate cortex; after taking power, it will raise the tone of the sympathetic system to an extreme, which will not be contained by the weak ventral vagal system. Thus, the neural resources that would allow the therapeutic bond to be created would be deactivated. In this situation, it would be impossible to make a connection; a fundamental aspect of the interaction must have the purpose of helping the child to remain regulated (Badenoch, 2017), in the intermediate zone that exists between the agitation promoted by the sympathetic and the disconnection promoted by the parasympathetic, within his window of tolerance (Schore, 2003). That is why it is important for the therapist to use resources that promote this regulated state.

The therapist turns to our child. The sweetness of his voice, his gentle manners and his smile contribute to producing a very different feeling from the one in the doctor's office.

The manners and gestures of the therapist have produced a calming effect thanks to interbody resonance (Fuchs, 2009). Recognising the emotional states of others depends on the imitative capacity of the brain. Thanks to mirror neurons, the brain reproduces the body attitude of the person with whom we are interacting as if we were adopting it. In this way, it informs us of the emotions or intentions of the other, influencing our emotional state at the same time (Ramseyer & Tschacher, 2014). When someone approaches us slowly, with arms relaxed at both sides of the body and a frank smile, the imitation of that state by our mirror neurons induces a state of openness and relaxation in us, deactivating neuroceptive states of fear.

The therapist delicately places his hand on the boy's shoulder and invites him to go to the room of the brave.

In addition to the visible body attitude, touch is a source of social cognition. It helps to recognise the state of mind of other people and synchronises one's body state with other's (Chatel-Goldman, Congedo, Jutten & Schwartz, 2014). It also produces profound changes in physiology and mental state, improving emotional regulation in children and adults (Grigorenko et al.,

2016; Grunwald, Weiss, Mueller & Rall, 2014), boosting feelings of security (Koole, Tjew A Sin & Schneider, 2014) and consolidating the bond between patient and therapist ((Montague, Chen, Xu, Chewning, & Barrett, 2013); Schroeder, Risen, Gino & Norton, 2014).

The child's senses, sharpened by the need to verify similarities and differences between the therapist and the doctor, transmit information that generates a neuroceptive state of security; delicate physical contact further attenuates the activity of the sympathetic system; furthermore, her own organism resonates with the therapist's calm and affectionate body attitude.

Informed about these discrepancies, the cingulate cortex changes the orientation of the possible harm/possible benefit balance and transfers its conclusions to the orbital area of the prefrontal cortex. This area is profusely connected with the subcortical nuclei of the limbic system, including the amygdala, on which it exerts a regulatory effect. The decrease in activation of the amygdala inverts the polarity of the ANS, intensifies the functioning of the parasympathetic system, specifically the ventral nucleus of the vagus, quickly but gently reducing the sympathetic influence. This nucleus is anatomically and functionally related to other nerve nodes from which cranial nerves originate, which are essential for the control of facial expression (cranial nerve VII, facial nerve) and head orientation (cranial nerve XI, accessory nerve). Together with them, it forms the ***ventral vagal complex*** (Porges, 2009), essential to promote the safe and attentive stillness necessary in the establishment of the social bond.

And finally, the sandtray: a source of instant emotional regulation

The room of the brave confirms the impression of friendliness, calm and safety perceived from the therapist. Nothing to do with the doctor's office. A large space, a comfortable chair for the patient and a small round table, letting the therapist sit close and at the patient's height, unlike in the doctor's office. Both the appearance of the therapist and the environment help to deactivate the neuroceptive state of threat in the child, make him feel safe and allow him to activate the social connection systems that release his neural resources and expand the range of tolerable perceptions and memories.

Suddenly, looking back to the right, a surprise. An army of miniatures are arranged in an orderly fashion on shelves that almost reach the ceiling. Its colours, its shapes and its great variety activate explicit memories associated with the game that make the child relive the pleasure of playing.

The neurobiological system of **pleasure** maintains the same characteristics in most mammals (Spear, 2011). It is very rich in **dopamine,** a neurotransmitter, and its response is similar regardless of the type of reward (an addictive substance, watching porn on the internet, playing games, a pat on the back...). From birth, it is ready to learn to enjoy experiences and distinguish which ones are the most enjoyable. In mammals, among other functions, the stimulation of reward circuits through play plays a stress-regulating role (Burgdorf, Kroes & Moskal, 2017).

As with the fear circuits, the pleasure circuits are also buried deep in the brain (see Figure 7.2). The **nucleus Accumbens**, somewhat smaller than its antagonist, the amygdala, and very close to it anatomically, is responsible for the "sensation of pleasure". Nearby, a neural network known as the **ventral striatum** is activated to detect stimuli that indicate the possibility of a reward; it also "warms up our engines", it motivates us, when we anticipate the pleasure we are going to receive. The relationship between these areas with the subcortical nuclei amygdala and the cingulate cortex (Bush et al., 2000) will contribute to establishing the risk/benefit balance that will finally give free rein to our opportunities to enjoy ourselves; or, on the contrary, it will extinguish the flame of desire. There is no chance of fully indulging in the pleasure of playing if the amygdala continues to give cause for alarm. In spite of everything, the strongest monitoring body depends on the functioning of the prefrontal cortex, where all the perceptual, neuroceptive and memory information, both implicit and explicit, is available. It will be the supreme judge who will finally decide whether it is worth taking the risk.

The child can only indulge in the pleasure of playing if the evolution of the aforementioned brain activity (amygdala/accumbens-cingulate-prefrontal-amygdala/accumbens and back again) declares victory, in shape of a neuroception of security and joy. If his previous history, retrieved through implicit and explicit memories, has strengthened your amygdala, and has developed a pessimistic advisor (the cingulate), more oriented towards overestimating possible harm than seeking pleasure, it will be more difficult for the accumbens to succeed. If the prefrontal cortex is weakened, it will resign and leave the course of events in the hands of the subcortical structures, which, in most cases, will opt for a rapid response aimed at avoiding damage by disregarding possible rewards. This rapid response will cause paralysis and disengagement if the vagus dorsalis-dependent parasympathetic system is activated, or fight and flight if the sympathetic system is activated. In neither of these two cases will it be possible to carry out a therapeutic encounter; for this to take place, it is necessary to achieve, as a previous step to the game, a good bond in a safe environment and a good capacity for emotional regulation in children who lack it.

The attitude of the therapist, as well as the opportunity to enjoy a bit of play, have made the child forget almost completely the black omens he felt by the door of the therapy room. This seems to be something else: a corrective experience with a therapeutic effect may occur (Ecker, Ticic & Hulley, 2012).

The game starts: body-limbic-prefrontal vertical integration

Encouraged by the child's excitement, the therapist decides to suggest creating a sandtray. He gently tells the child, "As you can see, on this shelf there are various items that represent symbols inhabiting the external and internal world of people".

The sight of the different objects and figures that fill the shelves bring up different memories. Each of them is related to different concepts. Perceptual memory helps to recognise and name them for what they are: a tree, a truck, a man, a woman. In addition, since memory is a task carried out by the whole brain, the memories corresponding to the meaning of the objects are also activated, thus introducing a higher level of complexity. Perceptual memory identifies a lorry, for example, it in all those figures in the shape of a large vehicle with large wheels; but semantic memory allows us to distinguish several types of lorry, according to their purpose: transport, firefighters, tanker. Finally, and simultaneously, the episodic memory attracts associated contents related to the times and places in which a lorry was seen or heard about. These episodic memories carry added meanings: the fire truck, for example, will bring up memories related to fire, danger, help and rescue.

As we have already discussed, the brain states associated with implicit memory are activated according to the contents evoked by explicit memories, providing the emotional soup from that gives them all their value. Following

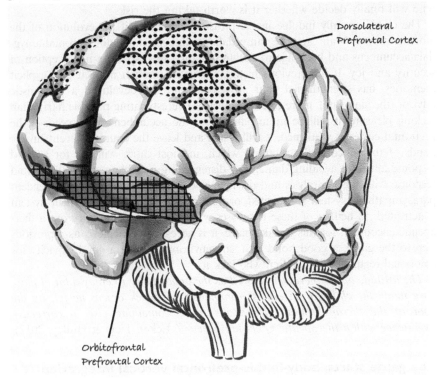

Figure 7.4 The prefrontal cortex is concerned with regulating the activity of the nervous system to achieve internally set goals

our example, it is difficult to contemplate a fire engine without simultaneously feeling the fear of fire, the joy at the possibility of receiving help or children's excitement associated with being a firefighter.

The child identifies some adult male figures: one is in a bathing suit, another is wearing work clothes, some are wearing a costume; but these are not the ones that most impress him. For our child, it is difficult to see figures of older men in suits without feeling implicit contents associated with the figure of his father: the chill, the feeling of nausea, the weakness in the legs and the fear.

The therapist continues to speak. "You just need to choose the items you like and place them in the sandtray; however you want, and to do whatever you want."

The evocation of the neuroceptive states that are part of the implicit memory arises unconsciously as soon as one contemplates the figures. Each of them refers to different perceptions, meanings and episodes; and also to the associated emotional/neuroceptive states. So, each one of them exerts an attractive effect on whoever makes the tray, to the extent that they are in tune with their implicit memories.

As soon as these instructions are received, the child gets down to work. As we have mentioned, the first phases of the task are initiated from subcortical nuclei and networks. The activation of the nuclei of pleasure sets the desire to play in motion as well as the motivation to do so; later, it will leave the task of selecting figures to the hands of implicit and explicit memories. So far, the stage has not yet been developed, let alone the story. To construct it, the cerebral cortex and the prefrontal cortex must collaborate.

Located in the foremost part of the brain, behind the forehead, above the eye sockets, the so-called prefrontal cortex has earned the title of "manager" or "conductor" of the brain. It has a complete map of the cerebral cortex, and it is also connected to all the subcortical nuclei we have mentioned. Its duty is to organise, regulate and direct the activity of the nervous system to free it from slavery to the most pressing and immediate needs (arising from subcortical and neuroceptive activity); as well as to subtract it from the attraction of the most remarkable sensory stimuli. Thanks to the prefrontal cortex, we manage to control the need for immediate gratification if we foresee a future reward of greater magnitude. It is responsible for keeping us faithful to the objective of the task by controlling possible interference from sensations or memories that are foreign to it. Thanks to the prefrontal cortex, we are able to escape from tangible reality by elaborating theories and hypotheses about how the world works and, more importantly, about the mental states of our fellow human beings.

The prefrontal cortex occupies a large area of the brain (see Figure 7.3; 7.4). It is connected to all areas of the brain and has a complete map of the entire cerebral cortex. We can distinguish three areas in it that seem to be specialised in different aspects of monitoring and regulating emotions and behaviour: the dorsolateral, the ventromedial and the orbitofrontal areas.

The dorsolateral zone of the prefrontal cortex (DLPFC) is in charge of keeping interesting mental contents alive, those that deserve attention based on the objectives of the task undertaken. It is the seat of a very particular form of memory that we have not described yet called working memory; in it, the necessary data to carry out the task at hand is retained, then it is deleted after using it, and the data needed for the next step is noted down. We use this type of memory to answer a question we were just asked, or to dial a phone number we were just told a few moments ago. The activity of the DLPFC is closely related to attention, motivation and cognitive flexibility (Monsell, 2003). It determines the focus of our attention because it helps us not to lose sight of the objective; it contributes to maintaining motivation because, thanks to the permanent incitement of the pleasure circuits, it supports brain function oriented towards achieving a goal (Miller & Cummings, 2013); and it makes attention more flexible precisely because of the provisional nature of its contents, which are deleted and replaced by others according to the needs of the moment (Monsell, 2003). Much of the sensation of the present is obtained from this form of memory since, after all, the present is the conjunction of the most recent past with the nearest future.

Neuroceptive states are constantly in our psychic life. In the form of implicit memories or reactions to current events, these physiological states, constantly monitored by the insula and limbic system, tell us the meaning of what we remember and what is happening, and how what is happening now is related to what happened then. It answers questions like "Am I feeling safer?", or "What will I feel if I do this?" The **VentroMedial area (VM PFC)** of the prefrontal cortex is activated whenever we face an emotional activity (MacNamara & Phan, 2018); it deals above all with internal states. Its activity does not imply ignoring the world, but precisely monitoring the way in which the environment affects us, the echo or resonance caused by what surrounds us. It plays an important role in identifying the mental states of others by detecting what they make us feel (Koenigs et al., 2007), that is, the neuroceptive states that they provoke in us. It also collaborates with the orbital zone of the prefrontal cortex to regulate our internal states. The VM PFC is in charge of extinguishing conditioned fear (Milad, Rosenbaum & Simon, 2014)(Kalisch et al., 2006). Its connection with the amygdala and the accumbens allows it to calculate intense and contradictory emotions that point us to divergent courses of action (MacNamara & Phan, 2018); this occurs, for example, in moral decisions, in which the VM PFC is especially involved (Nicolle & Goel, 2013). It is also closely connected to the hippocampus, to which it turns to request information about previous experiences that help in the decision (MacNamara & Phan, 2018). When this area of the PFC is damaged, our behaviour can become self-centred, devoid of any kind of consideration for others (Motzkin, Newman, Kiehl & Koenigs, 2011).

Any act produced by the activity of the nervous system is the result of a balance. The DL PFC stays on target, encouraged by the emotional states that the VM PFC is constantly recognising and regulating; but, at the same time, continuous stimuli are arising outside and within us that attract attention, and may be relevant (or not) to the achievement of the objective. In addition, we have a large number of memories to compare with the current situation before making a decision; each one of them will produce a different result in the risk/benefit balance operations of the cingulate cortex. **The orbitofrontal cortex (OF PFC)** is responsible for integrating the myriad of data and internal and external activations that we experience at each moment of mental activity; it controls possible interference from brain activations unrelated to the current task, keeps those that are relevant to it; it help us wait and inhibit the impulse to act at first (inhibition of pushy behaviour), taking into account past and present data to maximise profits and minimise losses (Balleine & O'Doherty, 2010). To put it simply: it prevents the predominant emotional states from becoming direct behaviours (Barbas, 2007). This is very convenient when immediate gratification must be foregone in order to achieve a higher profit in the future. It is so anatomically similar to the VM PFC that it is difficult to clearly separate them; and like the latter, it also deals with recognition and emotional modulation, although it is mostly responsible for its practical application and the actual performance of the behaviour (Kringelbach, 2005; Schoenbaum, Takahashi, Liu & Mcdannald, 2011).

Ever observant, the therapist perceives the child's doubt and corrections when choosing the sandtray figures. So, he encourages him: "If you don't know which items to choose, let it choose you. Let yourself go, don't think too much, let yourself flow".

The neuroceptive state and the two forms of memory oversee choosing the figures and objects that will serve to make the tray. The child digs into his memory looking for the story he wants to represent in the explicit memory section; each memory of data and facts carries the corresponding implicit content. The DL PFC starts, spurred on by the pleasure of the game and the desire to build the scene, channelling the emotions and memories processed by the VM PFC, trying to find the miniatures that awaken the closest emotional content to the one that is being evoked. The VM PFC, in contact with the insula, recognises what the child feels when observing the items and at the same time compares that neuroceptive state that arises when the implicit memories are evoked. The DL PFC maintains the information about the item to search for some time, according to the contents processed by the VM PFC; when the item is found, that information is deleted and replaced with the neuroceptive and memory cues that will guide the search for a new miniature or object. The idea of "letting the items choose the patient" reaches its full meaning here. The child notices the coincidence between his neuroceptive state and the sensation produced by the miniature as if he were experiencing some kind of magnetism, before even realising it. It is intuition, the hunch that is part of the unconscious wisdom that emanates from embodied cognition. Several experiments have confirmed that activations of the Autonomic Nervous System not consciously perceived guide our decisions when we do not have enough information about the way forward (Bechara et al., 1997; Tranel & Damasio, 1985; Denburg et al., 2009).

Although the need to describe the process intelligibly forces us to think of the brain functioning as a linear sequence, this is not really the case. There are different activation patterns competing at once to capture the collaboration of the same brain areas, so that the process occurs in a parallel way. For this reason, while the VM PFC and the DL PFC work together with neuroception and the memories to carry out the task, the OF PFC eliminates possible interferences (for example, thoughts like "what am I going to do when I get out of here?", or feelings like "I'm so hungry, I haven't eaten yet"); it controls the tendency to immediately choose the most attractive items because of their proximity, their size or their colour or because they arouse the most intense emotions; it modulates emotional states and impulses so as not to give in to the temptation to place the items randomly, and it keeps the spirit of searching alive in memory, not settling until the VM PFC believes that there is a match between what it sees and what it feels. Its contribution to emotional regulation facilitates the activity of the VM PFC, preventing it from suffering an emotional flood in which the "noise" does not allow us to distinguish the different "harmonics" of the affective melody.

The PFC relies on the ventral branch of the vagus which, mediating between the sympathetic and parasympathetic ends of the dorsal vagal nucleus, favours a state of attentive calm and full consciousness. The therapist's positive attitude and empathy activate it by generating a neuroception of safety. And finally, this is more and more empowered by stimulation of the OF PFC and , which need it to stay focused on the task.

Importance of the cerebral hemispheres

Despite already having a few miniatures in his hand, the child turns to the therapist for approval; he seems insecure, he wants to do well, get a good grade. Noticing this, with a smile, the therapist gives his patient one last important instruction: "Nothing can go wrong. What we want to see is exactly what you're going to make. This is a different experience from others you might have had: there is no judging or scoring". It is true, the child is going to make his world. His memory and neuroceptive sensations are evoking the necessary memory material; the PFC DL, excited by all those little toys, initiates and maintains the search. The child looks excitedly at the shelves full of miniatures. He does not know exactly what he is looking for, but his emotional state and memories give him some clues. Right now it is the right half of their brain, the right hemisphere, that is freely doing most of the work. The left hemisphere, the other half, must shut up.

As with other body organs, all brain structures and fascicles are duplicated in the cranial cavity on either side of a midline, partially separated by a sickle-shaped extension of the meninges. The duplicity present in systems such as the respiratory (two lungs) or the urinary (two kidneys) is both anatomical and functional. The right and left kidneys have the same structure and the same function except for a small difference in size between them. On superficial inspection, the two cerebral hemispheres appear to be the same. However, if we look at them in more detail, we discover differences in the size of some areas of the cortex: more volume of the prefrontal area in the right hemisphere and more size of the occipital area in the left hemisphere. Anatomical differences correspond to differences in the function they perform. It is said that each hemisphere is specialised for certain functions; but it is not exactly the case. Each one has its own way of approaching reality and its way of understanding it; the two take care of everything in different ways; as if we had two brains with different and complementary abilities, with two ways of understanding the world (McGilchrist, 2012).

One of the most common myths about the hemisphere is that the right one manages emotions, whereas the left one is thought of as cold accountant, only interested in precise and objective data. The reality is quite different. A meta-analysis does not recognise a hemispheric specialisation in managing emotions (Murphy, Nimmo-Smith & Lawrence, 2003). What happens is that the approach of the two halves of the brain to this issue is different: the right hemisphere is in charge of the emotional experience, of the embodied emotion; while the left one is essential to catalogue and tell what it feels like.

The child feels safe in the room of the brave and this frees up his brain functions to express themselves through play. He must "build a world" that reflects what he feels. Throughout his eleven years of age, he has sometimes felt scared, sometimes he has not. Some of the people most important to him have hurt, hit or insulted him, others have made him feel safer and have tried to protect him. He feels the need to put all this in the tray. As there are many miniatures and he still does not have a clear idea of what he is looking for, he uses his right hemisphere, which is much more capable of sustained, global and flexible attention. It is primarily the right VM PFC that takes over all the neuroceptive information and implicit memories about fear, harm, and safety. THE PCF DL maintains concentration and clearly writes "something scary" on its order board.

The right hemisphere is better at identifying the generic type of figures than each one in particular. If the PCF VM says, "this thing I feel/felt is fear" and the PCF DL constantly repeats "something scary, something scary", the right hemisphere looks for frightening figures, even if it is not able to name them; just as you would look for the shape of a tree regardless of species or type. One of the abilities of this half of the brain is to correlate internal states with events in the environment. It does not bring us closer to the world as a simple object of study; it always tries to understand its importance for us and our internal states. Its attention is drawn above all to figures in human form, objects that move as living beings do (Saxe, Xiao, Kovacs, Perrett & Kanwisher, 2004), and natural objects rather than tools (Gainotti, 2012).

When it finds the shelf with the monsters, it sees many and causing a different degree of fear; therefore, it presents the results to the left hemisphere so that it can start the process of detailed and analytical identification, as the left hemisphere is better at doing analysis and cataloguing. This time, the left PCF DL and the anterior area of the cingulate on the same side will contribute to this work of focus and identification. Their close relationship with the PCF OF helps them exploit the hippocampus to search throughout the brain, and especially in the visual cortex, for neuronal activations corresponding to the "monstrous" category of the identified figures. When it has confirmed it, it immediately sends its findings to the right hemisphere, which is in charge of establishing the correspondence between the effect produced by the figure, the implicit memory associated with it, and the neuroceptive state that is to be represented. The first choice is unsuccessful. It is a monster, yes, but the implicit and explicit memories evoked do not produce fear, but rather joy. The child remembers having a good laugh at that movie where this furry, horned individual had endless hilarious adventures with his mate, another monstrous, balloon-shaped, one-eyed being. The search resumes and refines. A new figure, it is the right one this time. The right hemisphere may be satisfied with a single figure if it is big enough and frightening enough. If not, it may keep looking or try to achieve the same effect by adding several with the same or similar aspects and expressions.

The task will always be easier if the figures are ordered and classified. Otherwise, the initial work, carried out mainly with the right hemisphere, will be interrupted by the constant requests from the left hemisphere to distinguish the figures. Hence, it is convenient to arrange the figures in an orderly manner in the therapy room. Later we will see that if the left hemisphere is awakened too early, much of the therapeutic work can be lost.

During this elaboration phase, the child keeps in mind the words of the therapist: *"Nothing can go wrong. What we want to see is exactly what you're going to make. This is a different experience from others you might have had: there is no judging or scoring"*. This has deactivated the natural tendency of the left hemisphere to interfere in the work of the right, as a kind of censor or editor, assessing the relevance of the content and its adaptation to canons or models from society and the cultural environment, or trying to impose a logical story, with a narrative composed of a beginning, a middle part and an ending. As we will see later, it is good for the right hemisphere to work alone on making the tray until it is finished, at which point the neighbour next door can be invited to look at the work.

The child continues his task looking for the correspondence between the activity of the right hemisphere and the subcortical activation patterns produced by the implicit and explicit memories. He now wants to place figures that reflect feelings of safety in the tray. In his life, there were experiences of terror and threatening presences, but also people and places that produced sensations of security and protection. The activity of the right hemisphere continues the search for figures related to these feelings; and once again, as many times as necessary, the collaboration of the left half is requested for the analysis of the findings. Once the elements have been chosen, the child prepares to place them inside the sandtray, thus converted into the translation from brain patterns, especially subcortical ones, corresponding to neuroceptions and implicit memories, made by his right hemisphere.

In this task, the right hemisphere probably takes on most of the work. It is more perceptive than the left when it comes to metaphors and jokes and has a much better ability to contextualise. That is why, while building a forest located between the monsters and the soldiers, he is not thinking of creating "an ecosystem formed by a group of trees" (as the left hemisphere would interpret it), but rather a fantastic place where fairies and goblins live, and protection and shelter can be found. The right hemisphere better manages the spatial relationships between objects and will direct the operations aimed at creating a scene that, when looked at, produces a pattern of brain activation that is overlaps the one that is represented. That feeling will produce a "eureka!" sensation (typical of this half of the brain) which will put an end to the task.

Not only does the cerebral cortex present two functionally differentiated halves; the rest of the nuclei mentioned so far are also duplicated: we have two hippocampi, two amygdalae and two accumbens. And research is beginning to reveal functional differences between them.

Exploring the sandtray: a vertical functioning, integrated horizontally

Elaborating the sandtray is non-linguistic work. In fact, not talking during the process is recommended. In most people, whether they are right-handed or left-handed, the left hemisphere oversees controlling the production and comprehension of a syntactically and grammatically correct language, paying particular attention to the internal logic of speech and the understanding of abstract concepts. Awakening this brain function while the right hemisphere is so busy bringing an internal world outward can contaminate its work or distract it.

When the job is done, the boy takes a step back, relaxes and contemplates his work.

The moments of silence that follow confirm the satisfaction of the right hemisphere and give time for the left to join in. We are looking at a representation of brain states created primarily by the right hemisphere of the child's brain with material provided by implicit and explicit memories. That sandtray is the container of an important part of the child's internal world and has its own rules. It is as it is and we must approach the scene by activating above all our right hemisphere: "opening" our perception to our own neuroceptive states. This is not the time to turn to the left side and impoverish the content of this childish message by analysing, discriminating, judging or imposing logical or grammatical rules. We will see why later. To facilitate the task, the therapist, who has so far stood in front of the child trying to watch the construction of the tray from the outside, now stands by the patients to contemplate this world as they see it. This way, the therapist's right hemisphere activity will tune in with the child's right hemisphere contents arranged in the tray.

Sometimes, the left hemisphere will overtake the right hemisphere's silence once their duty is done. Perhaps it will start to comment immediately, describing the scene with words. It knows no other way to expressing itself. Other times, the therapist will have to encourage it with a question. *"Do you want to tell me something about this world?"*

The left hemisphere is perfectly capable of building a story from the elements arranged in the tray. It knows what each element represents and interprets the internal logic of the scene according to the elements' features and their arrangement. The DL PFC constantly encourages it to stay focused and maintain the train of thought. Its VM PFC, together with the left amygdala, begins to consciously represent the catalogue of emotions and affection that, up to this point, were just an impressionistic image painted by the right hemisphere.

However, unlike the right hemisphere did during the elaboration phase, it struggles to work alone; it needs the other hemisphere to tell the story. If we could hear all the messages exchanged through the corpus callosum, we would hear the whisper of the right hemisphere trying to guide its neighbour, like a theatre prompter whispering lines to the actors, or simply silently nodding or denying while the other speaks. In this way, the right areas of the DL, OF and VM PFC agree or disagree with the work of their counterparts on the left side. Without this collaboration, the story would be meaningless to the patient, as if they were just reciting a previously memorised story. The left hemisphere writes good stories, but it needs the right to turn them into fascinating and unforgettable movies. This is the difference between the narrative that gives meaning to the experience pragmatically and authentically, and the intellectualised or rationalising discourse at the service of self-deception.

What the therapist sees is not simply the staging of an event, but the metaphorical representation of explicit memories (perceptual, episodic and semantic) and implicit memories, in the right hemisphere's peculiar style. It is an impressionistic style in which the scarcity of elements does not imply poverty of content; on the contrary, the metaphorical representation includes multiple meanings, some of them inaccessible to the narrative effort of the left hemisphere. However, the right hemisphere of the therapist will not miss them: they have the talent and the experience to identify them in the world in the tray and to offer them to the child using the analytical and linguistic skills of the left hemisphere.

It is not always necessary for the therapist to elicit some comment about the contents of the tray; but if they do, it should be in a way that contributes to the child's hemispheric integration. To achieve this, they should preferably ask questions instead of making statements; encouraging the recursive brain work that has allowed the realisation of the tray. Thus, after congratulating the boy for his work, the therapist asks: *"how do you think these soldiers feel?"* (see Figure 2.2 in Chapter 2). Would it not be the same for the therapist to say, *"it seems to me that these soldiers must be very scared"*? It would not, because it poses two problems: on the one hand, by speaking directly about the emotions of the soldiers, it would address the child's right hemisphere again, which is much more competent than the left in analysing the emotional shade of situations and relationships. Maintaining therapeutic work on only one side of the brain means losing the benefit of hemispheric integration, on which we will expand later; however, that statement is the result of the collaborative work of the therapist's cerebral hemispheres and does not necessarily match the mental contents of the child. The therapist's right hemisphere has become aware of the emotional and relational significance of the depicted scene by drawing on their own implicit and explicit memories related to the miniatures and their arrangement in the tray. In addition, it has information about the child's history. All these elements generate a constant exchange of information between the two hemispheres; an exchange parallel to the one that takes place in the child's brain while elaborating their sand world. By offering an interpretation, the therapist interrupts the dialogue between the child's cerebral hemispheres, making it difficult to integrate the child's mental contents and proposing the conclusions of a foreign brain that has been observing without really knowing the ins and outs of the process.

Let us go back to the question: *"How do you think these soldiers feel?"*. The question is decoded by the child's left hemisphere, in a place in the cortex called Wernicke's area, located at the back of the temporal lobe. The child's left hemisphere understands the question, but it does not know the answer as it has not made the tray: thus, it transfers it to the right hemisphere. That world is its work, it knows the answer. Perhaps at that moment the child's right hemisphere sighs in relief, with a feeling like *"Finally, my left neighbour on seems willing to listen to me. Well, I'm going to show it something it hasn't heard so far or has decided to ignore"*. It is much more in touch with neuroceptive states, with the world and with people. It is much more interested in reality and the human than the left, its feet are closer to the ground, to the sand, the same sand on which it has arranged the little figures. Its limitations depend precisely on its attachment to land, flesh and blood. It is difficult for it to fly over them, put them in perspective, see beyond the immediate and build consistent and structured narratives, useful for elaborating theories and abstractions made up of elements that can be manipulated. For that, it needs its partner's help, and it is the constant transfer of information from the right to the left hemisphere that allows to generate full consciousness by putting words to the ineffable, making room in history for the inexplicable. That is why after the therapist's question, a new exchange of information takes place between both sides of the brain: the left hemisphere will share the question with the right so that the latter asks the limbic system about its implicit content; when this responds, it will transfer the response to an area of the left hemisphere called Broca's area, where the response will occur. Left hemisphere, right hemisphere, limbic system, right hemisphere and left hemisphere. This is the sequence that enriches the narration and contributes to a better understanding of what is represented.

If we could listen to the conversation through the corpus callosum, we would hear the right hemisphere drawing the left hemisphere's attention to the enormous disproportion between the two sides. The monsters must be many more, much bigger and better armed. If the left hemisphere listens, it will complete the story with these new contributions, thus improving the possibilities of understanding and explaining the past situation and increasing the repertoire of future predictions. The capacity of the left PCF to operate with these new elements in a symbolic and virtual way offers a large number of alternatives to face the difficulties to come.

Unfortunately, the left hemisphere does not always want to listen. It is a journalist, an image consultant, not a historian. Their task is not to systematically accept the contents of the right neighbour on the right to operate with them, but in denying or distorting them when appropriate so that, as William Randolph Hearst said, "the truth does not spoil a good story". It has its reasons. In some cases, it lacks the ability to put words to the contents of the right hemisphere. This happens, for example, in the first years of development, when it has not yet developed all its linguistic capacity; although this is not the case of our child, who has enough lexical and grammatical resources at 11 years of age. The other, far more common reason is that it does not seem possible or convenient to translate the content transmitted from the right hemisphere because it is UNSPEAKABLE, unbearably terrifying, very threatening or deathly sad. And in this case the child (or better, their right hemisphere) has clearly represented their feelings of helplessness despite the help received. Faced with these emotions, the left hemisphere only has two alternatives: the *"Disney tactic"* or the *"Religion strategy"*. If the first one is chosen, the story will be built ignoring everything that can be related to emotionally indigestible content: sex, crime, the meaninglessness of death, the suffering of the innocent... If the second is chosen, complex stories with happy ending will be elaborated, that reassure the listener and make them feel that everything is explained.

Sometimes the left hemisphere opts for a third way: it simply stays quiet. The child will then say that they prefer not to talk about their world and forcing them would be a mistake. Insisting would stimulate the activity of the right hemisphere and make it scream louder and louder, catching the left hemisphere's attention. The latter would cover its ears because it cannot explain, or it has good reasons not to do so. As no relief is offered through language, the child's neuroceptive state would become increasingly unmanageable, leading to a situation close to dissociation (alternating, non-integrated functioning of the right and left hemispheres, Teicher et al., 2004) (Popkirov, Flasbeck, Schlegel, Juckel & Brüne, 2018) or impulsive dyscontrol (resignation of the left hemisphere and emotional hijacking due to the impossibility of the right PCF to manage subcortical activation without help, Kamphausen et al., 2013; Lang et al., 2012; Schmahl, Vermetten, Elzinga & Douglas Bremner, 2003).

Through the co-exploration phase, the therapist's questions stimulate the collaborative and integrative work of the two halves of the child's brain, improving their understanding of the situations experienced and providing tools that will help them in the future.

How and when to end the game

Once the co-exploration phase is over, it is convenient to return to reality without abruptness. While making the tray, the patient has placed their brain states in the constructed world, and we have tried to work from within them to facilitate the work of hemispheric integration that we have so far illustrated. Redirecting the attentional systems towards reality too quickly will suddenly interrupt the dialogue between the brain halves, preventing them from reaching a state of reconciliation. As if a mediator hastily concluded the discussion between the parties in conflict without having achieved some form of agreement or even the hope of obtaining it. By calmly and gradually completing the task, the right hemisphere may feel that it has taught the left something new, and the left has been able to integrate what it has learned into its narrative.

Before collecting the tray, we can suggest taking a photo. The convenience of doing so has to do with a characteristic of our memory: remembering implies reconstructing, partially modifying what is remembered. Trying to remember the contents of a certain tray implies a call to visual memory, in which the prefrontal cortex and the hippocampus will participate with the inevitable activation of the visual cortex located in the occipital lobe. This memory will be inevitably accompanied by the neuroceptive state that was implicitly recorded as a pattern of subcortical brain activation. The association of these two forms of memory, implicit and explicit, imposes changes because emotions strengthened certain memories, but could also mark others as threatening, harmful or harmful. Hence, the reconstruction entails empowering certain elements and possibly censoring or distorting others.

Taking photographs helps to correct these deformations, making the effort of the left hemisphere to rebuild the tray useless. The evidence does not allow it to display its narrative creativity at the expense of the testimony provided by the right hemisphere.

Care must be taken when a minor or an adult, unaware of the importance of the method, asks to take a photo to show it. They do not realise that it is going to show a part of their cerebral/mental states that is intimate and profound, hitherto unknown even to themselves and obviously to others.

The way the patient collects the tray is a good indicator of the extent to which they have achieved their goal. Dismantling this externalised internal world and returning the figures to their original position will tell us if peace has been achieved between these two partners. If they have, they will collect with harmony, giving preference to certain contents, delicately treating the figures as a reflection of their integrated neuronal activity; otherwise, they may refuse to pick it up (perhaps because the right hemisphere does not feel understood) or do so carelessly or angrily (when the left does not want to understand).

After shaking hands and under the direction of the therapist, both hemispheres can return their attention to reality to continue performing their usual tasks in the child's life.

Different ways to make neural networks work

Patient work styles

The sandtray is a multimodal therapeutic technique in which different contents are worked on at the same time. Depending on the way in which the patient uses the elements of the tray and on the type of suggestions or instructions of the therapist, three general kinds of work are distinguished: physical, emotional and intellectual-cognitive.

The **physical work** is aimed at focusing the patient's attention on the sensory experiences produced by contact with the sand and the shapes and colours of the figures. In these contents, the work of the cerebral cortex is limited to receiving the information detected by the organs of sight and touch, locating its origin. Tactile experiences such as that produced when playing with sand improve emotional regulation in children and adults (Grunwald et al., 2014; Leonard, Berkowitz & Shusterman, 2014) and contribute to improving the feeling of trust and safety (Koole et al., 2014). Free play with sand and figures does not require the right hemisphere to work with problematic emotional content, nor does it require the left hemisphere to elaborate a narrative about it. Stimulation of the tactile C fibres is achieved, specialised in collecting stimuli that have the quality that we associate with caresses.

Emotional work is typical of the right hemisphere. Not so much because it is the cerebral side of emotions, but because of its specialisation in establishing connections between the environment and our internal states. Despite everything, as we have already discussed, it requires the collaboration of the left hemisphere to home in on the choice of items.

Finally, the intellectual-cognitive work adds the co-exploration phase to the elaboration of the box (a mostly emotional process), seeking the participation of the left hemisphere to recognise and integrate content presented by the right hemisphere. As we have previously illustrated, some of these contents come as a surprise to the left hemisphere which, due to deafness or a refusal to listen, has decided to exclude them from the story.

Some patients finish the tray right away, relatively quickly for the emotional intensity of the task. Such speed reminds us of when common behavioural programs such as driving a car or riding a bicycle are learned and developed. It is also typical of brief, superficial social contacts focused on forms rather than on the development of an intimate affective relationship. When the task is performed quickly, we should suspect a scant participation of the right hemisphere and the implementation of brain patterns commanded by the left hemisphere, much more accustomed to developing stereotyped, learned, formally logical and consistent narratives but devoid of a connection with the internal state.

In other cases, the speed depends on a runaway and disorganised activity of the right hemisphere, very common in patients with difficulties in emotional regulation. Although it is more connected to the internal state, from which emotions emanate, the right hemisphere is not as efficient as the left when it comes to cooling down affection. We have discussed how, while making the tray, the left side of the brain constantly intervenes to refine the choice of miniatures; but this is not its only mission during the process. Its greater connection with the parasympathetic (vagal) system tries to maintain the state of emotional activation at a tolerable intensity that does not turn the behaviour into a mere rapid and disorganised expulsion of content.

At the other end of the spectrum, we have patients who take too long. Sometimes they have a hard time choosing the figures; sometimes they seem doubtful, they cannot make up their minds clearly about any of them, or they even change them constantly during the process. It may be an attention problem. Dysfunction of the prefrontal cortex, especially in the right dorsolateral area, markedly impairs maintenance of attention. For those who seem disoriented by the large number of miniatures and move in front of the shelf without focusing their gaze, a right hemisphere deficit is more likely. When problems depend on the left, we are more likely to see good initial focused attention followed by continuous doubts, changes and interruptions. This is the case of patients who, for example, show a clear preference for the type of figures tuned to their internal state, but lack detailed perception typical of the left hemisphere, which is necessary to confirm a certain choice. These difficulties depend on communication problems between both hemispheres; either because the pathways of the corpus callosum are not well developed, or because the left hemisphere is somewhat hard of hearing, it is difficult for it to recognise the contents presented by the right one, or it has reasons to impose its criteria.

Two ways to introduce work with the sandbox

Depending on the way in which the therapist poses the realisation of the tray, we can distinguish two working methods. Each one of them poses the beginning of two different neural processes, with different therapeutic properties, each applicable to specific situations.

Non-directive method

The therapist can suggest making the tray without a specific goal or theme, leaving the patient free to build the world as they wish. This freedom of choice makes the therapeutic sense of the task seemingly disappear, stimulating above all the playful nature of the technique. Taken as play, the performance of the sandtray makes the fascicles and nuclei related to pleasure run freely, and it is they that provide the fuel that sustain behaviour. Even if implicit and explicit memory contents associated with trauma come up, they are less likely to arouse fearful amygdalar reactions that hinder the task as intense activity of the accumbens reduces that of the amygdala and hippocampus. During play, the cingulate cortex does not receive any information that anticipates pain or loss; nor is there any expectation regarding the result, as the therapist does not expect anything specific from the patient, and the patient does not have to follow a specific theme. The left hemisphere will then collaborate with the right hemisphere, fine-tuning the choices without placing any restrictions on what is appropriate, accurate or relevant. A field is opened for the creativity and imagination of the right hemisphere. The pleasure of playing anticipated by the accumbens, the reduction in anxiety associated with low amygdala activity, the favourable balance of the cingulate, and the relaxation of left hemisphere sensory activity make the nondirective method a convenient procedure for patients with a history of severe trauma or emotional regulation difficulties; especially when they have not yet done therapeutic work that prepares them to better tolerate and regulate their emotions.

This does not turn the free, non-directive tray into a task empty of useful content for therapy. Rather, it is about promoting a **positive dissociation** in which the patient is not deceived, but rather attenuates brain activations that could hinder or contaminate the result, causing defensive reactions or episodes of emotional or behavioural lack of control. If a patient who has not yet advanced in therapy is asked to represent traumatic contents (implicit and explicit memories associated with the trauma, amygdala hyperactivity, anticipation of damage by the cingulate and defensive operations of the left hemisphere), brain states are produced that make integrated functioning difficult and prevent from processing the traumatic experience.

Without the restrictions that this lack of integration would cause, the right hemisphere unfolds freely, transferring the internal states detected to the tray, without the pressure implied in having to stick to a topic or satisfying the therapist's request. The patient's brain is in "game mode" and the objective of their behaviour is to simply transfer their world to the tray. This is pleasant for the right hemisphere, interested above all in finding a match between what it feels and what it sees, regardless of its relationship with past or present real events. The left hemisphere will collaborate as described, occasionally contributing with its judgment, but most of the time it will be disconnected, without restricting the task and without imposing a tricky narrative.

It is the therapist who keeps their two hemispheres and their memory permanently connected and integrated. For the patient's brain it is "just a game", that is why the brain areas and connections related to fear and damage have been attenuated, and that is why the defensive operations of the left hemisphere have been deactivated. But the therapist makes the connections for them, using their knowledge of the patient, their therapeutic experience and their powers of observation to craft a narrative that makes sense of the created world and generates illuminating questions during the co-exploration phase.

Directive method

In the directive sandtray the central theme of the world elaborated by the patient is defined by themselves or by the therapist. It can revolve around a specific event, or it can be aimed at representing an idea or an emotion; it can be related to past events or to a forecast of the future.

The proposed theme will determine the type of brain functions used, and constant communication between both cerebral hemispheres will always be necessary. The fundamental difference with the non-directive tray is that the thematic delimitation calls for the participation of the left hemisphere from the beginning. This will make sure that the patient sticks to the theme, will collaborate in the construction of a story and sometimes undermine the freedom of the right hemisphere to create according to its activations. Hence, it is more useful in patients who have already done some therapy since they have managed to feel sufficiently safe in the sessions and have paved the way for effective emotional regulation and fluid interhemispheric communication.

When the patient's self is present in the tray

The patient can include themselves in the constructed world upon instruction of the therapist or out of their own will. But would that really be about them, about all of them? Sometimes one of the figures can actually be a representation of the ideal or real self; but other times, when the patient refers to a miniature or to a certain aspect of the tray as if it were themselves, they are actually speaking about a part of themselves. Let us remember that the tray world is built by transferring thoughts, memories, sensations and emotions that are already in the mind of the individual and make up their personality; so it is most likely that the tray world contains different parts of it, or only some of them.

Our personal characteristics, what defines our personality, our identity, is constituted by the particular forms of internal dialogue between the different brain areas within each hemisphere and the communication of both hemispheres with each other. The tray world can represent states of the self, states of the nervous system or partial aspects of its operation. A fragment of the represented scene may correspond to the interaction between, for example, the prefrontal cortex and the amygdala; or it can reproduce a certain brain state.

The tray world is built with elements from implicit memory (autonomic and limbic activation) and explicit memory (hippocampus) through the collaborative activity of both hemispheres. Therefore, each of these elements is a part of the mental activity itself. When the patient identifies with one of them, what they are doing is focusing on one of their mental contents or the relationship between some of them, rather than assigning a role to themselves; perhaps the most significant at the time of production (non-directive tray) or the most important for the subject matter (directive tray).

Conclusion

The sandbox is a powerful therapeutic tool for children and adults. Thanks to the playful nature of the activity, the pleasure circuits (system accumbens/ventral tegmental substance) are stimulated, and the anxiety related to the content of the sessions, full of often ineffable traumatic memories, is calmed down. If we approached them through language, the left hemisphere, managing everything related to the construction of discourse, would dominate, bypass the contents of implicit memory and carry out defensive operations by elaborating a logical but tricky narrative.

The tray world is a job that favours the vertical integration of the nervous system. While choosing the figures, and also during the elaboration phase, the prefrontal cortex must pay attention to the implicit evocations of the limbic system and listen to the body reactions to verify the match between what is remembered and what has been experienced. The therapist's instructions ("*You should just choose the items that appeal to you and place them in the sandtray as you wish, and to make whatever you want*") intensifies the need to divert attention to internal states, opening the insula and the right hemisphere to the perception of neuroceptive states. This refines the match between what the patient wants to represent and what the world looks like in the tray. At the same time, the excitement and pleasure produced by the game exert a constant emotional regulation effect. Thus, making the scene almost automatically contributes to maintaining vertical integration.

This therapeutic technique also facilitates horizontal integration. The construction of tray world mainly starts from the right hemisphere; but it has the intermittent and necessary collaboration of the left hemisphere, which remains oblivious to the task in most of the elaboration phase. The therapist encourages this temporal division (*"Nothing can go wrong. What we want to see is exactly what you're going to make. This is a different experience from others you might have had: there is no judging or scoring"*). This generates a transitory state of dissociation, of lack of integration in brain functioning, which prevents deregulated emotional states from appearing. Little by little, unnoticed by the patient, the implicit and explicit memories take shape outside their brain without eliciting defensive reactions or the construction of tricky stories, often elaborated by the left hemisphere.

When the task is finished and patient and therapist are contemplating the tray, the left hemisphere comes to life, makes contact with what it sees and begins to co-operate with the right hemisphere to build a story that facilitates the assimilation of the scene; sometimes spontaneously, in silence, other times with the collaboration of the therapist in the co-exploration phase. A phase in which the co-operation and exchange of information between hemispheres is requested in a co-ordinated and respectful way. This work offers the patient's brain the chance to incorporate contents into its narrative that until then were only felt or acted on, but not thought or verbalised. After the dissociation reintegration takes place, in which many of the contents have undergone modifications, have been stripped of their terrifying quality and have been better understood.

In this sense, the sandtray provides a space for emotional containment and regulation, in which implicit and explicit mental contents can be expressed through a medium that brings them back in a corrected and completed version, providing a deeper and more manageable knowledge of them.

References

Badenoch, B. (2017). *The heart of trauma: Healing the embodied brain in the context of relationships.* W.W. Norton & Company.

Balleine, B.W. & O'Doherty, J.P. (2010). Human and rodent homologies in action control: corticostriatal determinants of goal-directed and habitual action. *Neuropsychopharmacology: Official Publication of the American College of Neuropsychopharmacology, 35*(1), 48–69. doi:10.1038/npp.2009.131.

Barbas, H. (2007). Specialized elements of orbitofrontal cortex in primates. *Annals of the New York Academy of Sciences, 1121*(1), 10–32. doi:10.1196/annals.1401.015.

Bechara, A., Damasio, H., Tranel, D. & Damasio, A.R. (1997). Deciding advanta-
geously before knowing the advantageous strategy. *Science (New York, N.Y.)*, 275
(5304), 1293–1295. Retrieved from www.ncbi.nlm.nih.gov/pubmed/9036851.

Botvinick, M.M., Cohen, J.D. & Carter, C.S. (2004). Conflict monitoring and anterior
cingulate cortex: an update. *Trends in Cognitive Sciences*, 8(12), 539–546.
doi:10.1016/J.TICS.2004.10.003.

Boukezzi, S. et al. (2017). Grey matter density changes of structures involved in Posttraumatic Stress Disorder (PTSD) after recovery following Eye Movement Desensitization and Reprocessing (EMDR) therapy. *Psychiatry Research–Neuroimaging*,
266, 146–152. doi:10.1016/j.pscychresns.2017.06.009.

Burgdorf, J., Kroes, R.A. & Moskal, J.R. (2017). Rough-and-tumble play induces
resilience to stress in rats. *NeuroReport*, 1. doi:10.1097/WNR.0000000000000864.

Bush, G., Luu, P., Posner, M.I. & Posner, M. (2000). *Cognitive and emotional influences in anterior cingulate cortex.*

Chatel-Goldman, J., Congedo, M., Jutten, C. & Schwartz, J.-L. (2014). Touch increases autonomic coupling between romantic partners. *Frontiers in Behavioral Neuroscience*, 8(March), 95. doi:10.3389/fnbeh.2014.00095.

Chen, L., Zhang, G., Hu, M. & Liang, X. (2015). Eye Movement Desensitization and
Reprocessing Versus Cognitive-Behavioral Therapy for Adult Posttraumatic Stress
Disorder. *The Journal of Nervous and Mental Disease*, 203(6), 443–451. doi:10.1097/
NMD.0000000000000306.

Dale, L.P., Carroll, L.E., Galen, G., Hayes, J.A., Webb, K.W. & Porges, S.W. (2009).
Abuse history is related to autonomic regulation to mild exercise and psychological
wellbeing. *Applied Psychophysiology Biofeedback*, 34(4), 299–308. doi:10.1007/
s10484-009-9111-4.

Damasio, A. (2020). *El extraño orden de las cosas.* Barcelona: Destino.

Damasio, A.R. (2011). *El error de Descartes la emoción, la razón y el cerebro humano.*
Barcelona: Destino.

Denburg, N.L., Jones, R.D. & Tranel, D. (2009). Recognition without awareness in a
patient with simultanagnosia. *International Journal of Psychophysiology: Official
Journal of the International Organization of Psychophysiology*, 72(1), 5–12.
doi:10.1016/j.ijpsycho.2008.02.012.

Eagleman, D. (2013). *Incógnito: las vidas secretas del cerebro.* Barcelona.

Eagleman, D.M. & Holcombe, A.O. (2002). Causality and the Perception of Time.
Trends in Cognitive Sciences, 6(8), 323–325.

Ecker, B., Ticic, R. & Hulley, L. (2012). Unlocking the emotional brain: Eliminating
symptoms at their roots using memory reconsolidation. *Unlocking the Emotional
Brain: Eliminating Symptoms at Their Roots Using Memory Reconsolidation*, 1–244.
doi:10.4324/9780203804377.

Eisenberger, N.I., Lieberman, M.D. & Williams, K.D. (2003). Does rejection hurt? An
FMRI study of social exclusion. *Science (New York, N.Y.)*, 302(5643), 290–292.
doi:10.1126/science.1089134.

Ferry, B., Wirth, S. & Di Scala, G. (1999). Functional interaction between entorhinal
cortex and basolateral amygdala during trace conditioning of odor aversion in the
rat. *Behavioral Neuroscience*, 113(1), 118–125. Retrieved from www.ncbi.nlm.nih.
gov/pubmed/10197911.

Fuchs, T. (2009). Embodied cognitive neuroscience and its consequences for psychiatry. *Poiesis & Praxis*, 6(3), 219–233. doi:10.1007/S10202-008-0068-9.

Gainotti, G. (2012). Brain structures playing a crucial role in the representation of tools in humans and non-human primates. *Behavioral and Brain Sciences*, 35(4), 224–225. doi:10.1017/S0140525X11001890.

Gehring, W.J. & Fencsik, D.E. (2001). Functions of the medial frontal cortex in the processing of conflict and errors. *The Journal of Neuroscience: The Official Journal of the Society for Neuroscience*, 21(23), 9430–9437. doi:10.1523/JNEUROSCI.21-23-09430.2001.

Green, K.T. et al. (2016). Exploring the relationship between posttraumatic stress disorder symptoms and momentary heart rate variability. *Journal of Psychosomatic Research*, 82, 31–34. doi:10.1016/j.jpsychores.2016.01.003.

Grigorenko, E.L. et al. (2016). Epigenetic regulation of cognition: A circumscribed review of the field. *Development and Psychopathology*, 91(8), 1–20. doi:10.1017/S0954579416000857.

Grunwald, M., Weiss, T., Mueller, S. & Rall, L. (2014). EEG changes caused by spontaneous facial self-touch may represent emotion regulating processes and working memory maintenance. *Brain Research, 1557*, 111–126. doi:10.1016/j.brainres.2014.02.002.

Havas, D.A., Glenberg, A.M., Gutowski, K.A., Lucarelli, M.J. & Davidson, R.J. (2010). Cosmetic use of botulinum toxin-a affects processing of emotional language. *Psychological Science*, 21(7), 895–900. doi:10.1177/0956797610374742.

Hennenlotter, A., Dresel, C., Castrop, F., Ceballos-Baumann, A.O., Wohlschlager, A. M., Haslinger, B. & Haslinger, B. (2009). The Link between Facial Feedback and Neural Activity within Central Circuitries of Emotion–New Insights from Botulinum Toxin-Induced Denervation of Frown Muscles. *Cerebral Cortex*, 19(3), 537–542. doi:10.1093/cercor/bhn104.

Herrera Ortiz, A.F., Rincón Cuenca, N.T. & Fernández Beaujon, L. (2021). Brain Changes in Magnetic Resonance Imaging Caused by Child Abuse a Systematic Literature Review. *SSRN Electronic Journal*, (April). doi:10.2139/ssrn.3829917.

Kalisch, R., Korenfeld, E., Stephan, K.E., Weiskopf, N., Seymour, B. & Dolan, R.J. (2006). Context-dependent human extinction memory is mediated by a ventromedial prefrontal and hippocampal network. *The Journal of Neuroscience: The Official Journal of the Society for Neuroscience*, 26(37), 9503–9511. doi:10.1523/JNEUROSCI.2021-06.2006.

Kamphausen, S. et al. (2013). Medial prefrontal dysfunction and prolonged amygdala response during instructed fear processing in borderline personality disorder. *World Journal of Biological Psychiatry*, 14(4), 307–318. doi:10.3109/15622975.2012.665174.

Kandel, E.R., Kupfermann, I. & Iversen, S. (2000). Learning and memory. *Principles of neural science* (pp. 1227–1246). https://doi.org/10.1016/B978-0-444-53497-2.00055-3.

Killcross, S., Robbins, T.W. & Everitt, B. J. (1997). Different types of fear-conditioned behaviour mediated by separate nuclei within amygdala. *Nature*, 388(6640), 377–380. doi:10.1038/41097.

Koenigs, M., Young, L., Adolphs, R., Tranel, D., Cushman, F., Hauser, M. & Damasio, A. (2007). Damage to the prefrontal cortex increases utilitarian moral judgements. *Nature*, 446(7138), 908–911. doi:10.1038/nature05631.

Koole, S.L., Tjew ASin, M. & Schneider, I.K. (2014). Embodied Terror Management. *Psychological Science*, 25(1), 30–37. doi:10.1177/0956797613483478.

Kringelbach, M.L. (2005). The human orbitofrontal cortex: linking reward to hedonic experience. *Nature Reviews Neuroscience*, 6(9), 691–702. doi:10.1038/nrn1747.

Landin-Romero, R., Moreno-Alcazar, A., Pagani, M. & Amann, B.L. (2018). How Does Eye Movement Desensitization and Reprocessing Therapy Work? A Systematic Review on Suggested Mechanisms of Action. *Frontiers in Psychology*, 9, 1395. doi:10.3389/fpsyg.2018.01395.

Lang, S., Kotchoubey, B., Frick, C., Spitzer, C., Grabe, H.J. & Barnow, S. (2012). Cognitive reappraisal in trauma-exposed women with borderline personality disorder. *NeuroImage*, 59(2), 1727–1734. doi:10.1016/j.neuroimage.2011.08.061.

Leonard, J.A., Berkowitz, T. & Shusterman, A. (2014). The effect of friendly touch on delay-of-gratification in preschool children. *The Quarterly Journal of Experimental Psychology*, 67(11), 2123–2133. doi:10.1080/17470218.2014.907325.

MacNamara, A. & Phan, K.L. (2018). Neurocircuitry of Affective, Cognitive, and Regulatory Systems. In C. Schmahl & K.L. Phan (Eds), *Neurobiology of Personality Disorders* (pp. 3–38). New York: Oxford University Press.

Malter Cohen, M., Jing, D., Yang, R.R., Tottenham, N., Lee, F.S. & Casey, B.J. (2013). Early-life stress has persistent effects on amygdala function and development in mice and humans. *Proceedings of the National Academy of Sciences of the United States of America*, 110(45), 18274–18278. doi:10.1073/pnas.1310163110.

McGilchrist, I. (2012). *The Master and His Emissary: The Divided Brain and the Making of the Western World*.

McLaughlin, K.A., Rith-Najarian, L., Dirks, M.A. & Sheridan, M.A. (2015). Low Vagal Tone Magnifies the Association Between Psychosocial Stress Exposure and Internalizing Psychopathology in Adolescents. *Journal of Clinical Child and Adolescent Psychology*, 44(2), 314–328. doi:10.1080/15374416.2013.843464.

Méndez-Bértolo, C. et al. (2016). A fast pathway for fear in human amygdala. *Nature Neuroscience*, 19(8), 1041–1049. doi:10.1038/nn.4324.

Milad, M.R., Rosenbaum, B.L. & Simon, N.M. (2014). Neuroscience of fear extinction: Implications for assessment and treatment of fear-based and anxiety related disorders. *Behaviour Research and Therapy*, 62, 17–23. https://doi.org/10.1016/J.BRAT.2014.08.006.

Miller, B.J. & Cummings, J.L. (2013). *The Human Frontal Lobes* (2nd ed.). New York: Guilford Press.

Monsell, S. (2003). Task switching. *Trends in Cognitive Sciences*, 7(March), 134–140. doi:10.1016/S1364-6613(03)00028–00027.

Montague, E., Chen, P., Xu, J., Chewning, B. & Barrett. (2013). Nonverbal Interpersonal Interactions in Clinical Encounters and Patient Perceptions of Empathy. *J Participat Med*, 12(5), 1–18.

Moore, K.L., Dalley, A.F. & Agur, A.M.R. (2013). *Clinically Oriented Anatomy*. Lippincott Williams and Wilkins.

Motzkin, J.C., Newman, J.P., Kiehl, K.A. & Koenigs, M. (2011). Reduced prefrontal connectivity in psychopathy. *The Journal of Neuroscience: The Official Journal of the Society for Neuroscience*, 31(48), 17348–17357. doi:10.1523/JNEUROSCI.4215-11.2011.

Murphy, F.C., Nimmo-Smith, I. & Lawrence, A.D. (2003). Functional neuroanatomy of emotions: a meta-analysis. *Cognitive, Affective & Behavioral Neuroscience*, 3(3), 207–233. doi:10.3758/CABN.3.3.207.

Nicolle, A. & Goel, V. (2013). What is the role of the ventromedial prefrontal cortex in emotional influences on reason? *Emotion and Reasoning*, 154–173. doi:10.4324/9781315888538.

Niedenthal, P.M., Winkielman, P., Mondillon, L. & Vermeulen, N. (2009). Embodiment of emotion concepts. *Journal of Personality and Social Psychology*, 96(6), 1120–1136. doi:10.1037/a0015574.

O'Doherty, D.C.M., Chitty, K.M., Saddiqui, S., Bennett, M.R. & Lagopoulos, J. (2015). A systematic review and meta-analysis of magnetic resonance imaging measurement of structural volumes in posttraumatic stress disorder. *Psychiatry Research–Neuroimaging*, Vol. 232(30 April), 1–33. doi:10.1016/j.pscychresns.2015.01.002.

Popkirov, S., Flasbeck, V., Schlegel, U., Juckel, G. & Brüne, M. (2018). Childhood trauma and dissociative symptoms predict frontal EEG asymmetry in borderline personality disorder. *Journal of Trauma & Dissociation*, 1–16. doi:10.1080/15299732.2018.1451808.

Porges, S.W. (2009). The polyvagal theory: new insights into adaptive reactions of the autonomic nervous system. *Cleveland Clinic Journal of Medicine, 76*(Suppl 2), S86–90. doi:10.3949/ccjm.76.s2.17.

Porges, S.W. (2017). *La Teoria Polivagal: Fundamentos Neurofisiologicos De Las Emociones, El Apego, La Comunicacion Y La Autorregulacion*. Pleyades.

Ramseyer, F. & Tschacher, W. (2014). Nonverbal synchrony of head- and body-movement in psychotherapy: different signals have different associations with outcome. *Frontiers in Psychology*, 5. doi:10.3389/fpsyg.2014.00979.

Saxe, R., Xiao, D.K., Kovacs, G., Perrett, D.I. & Kanwisher, N. (2004). A region of right posterior superior temporal sulcus responds to observed intentional actions. *Neuropsychologia*, 42(11), 1435–1446. doi:10.1016/j.neuropsychologia.2004.04.015.

Schacter, D.L. & Wagner, A.D. (2013). Learning and Memory. Chapter 65 In E.R. Kandel, J.H. Schwartz, T.M. Jessell, S.A. Siegelbaum & A.J. Hudspeth (Eds), *Principles of Neural Science* (5th ed.). McGrawHill.

Schmahl, C.G., Vermetten, E., Elzinga, B.M. & Douglas Bremner, J. (2003). Magnetic resonance imaging of hippocampal and amygdala volume in women with childhood abuse and borderline personality disorder. *Psychiatry Research*, 122(3), 193–198. doi:10.1016/s0925-4927(03)00023–00024.

Schoenbaum, G., Takahashi, Y., Liu, T.L. & Mcdannald, M.A. (2011). Does the orbitofrontal cortex signal value? *Annals of the New York Academy of Sciences, 1239*(1), 87–99. doi:10.1111/j.1749-6632.2011.06210.x.

Schore, A.N. (2003). *Affect Regulation and the Repair of the Self* (1st ed.). W.W. Norton & Co.

Schroeder, J., Risen, J., Gino, F. & Norton, M.I. (2014). Handshaking Promotes Cooperative Dealmaking. *SSRN Electronic Journal*. doi:10.2139/ssrn.2443674.

Siegel, D. (2007). *La mente en desarrollo: Cómo interactúan las relaciones y el cerebro para modelar nuestro ser* (3rd ed.). Desclée de Brouwer.

Spear, L.P. (2011). Rewards, aversions and affect in adolescence: Emerging convergences across laboratory animal and human data. *Developmental Cognitive Neuroscience*, 1(October), 390–403. doi:10.1016/j.dcn.2011.08.001.

Szpunar, K.K., Watson, J.M. & McDermott, K.B. (2007). Neural substrates of envisioning the future. *Proceedings of the National Academy of Sciences of the United States of America*, 104(2), 642–647. doi:10.1073/pnas.0610082104.

Teicher, M.H., Dumont, N.L., Ito, Y., Vaituzis, C., Giedd, J.N. & Andersen, S.L. (2004). Childhood neglect is associated with reduced corpus callosum area. *Biological Psychiatry*, 56(2), 80–85. doi:10.1016/j.biopsych.2004.03.016.

Teicher, M.H. & Samson, J.A. (2016). Annual Research Review: Enduring neurobiological effects of childhood abuse and neglect. *Journal of Child Psychology and Psychiatry, and Allied Disciplines*, 57(3), 241–266. doi:10.1111/jcpp.12507.

Teicher, M.H., Samson, J.A., Anderson, C.M. & Ohashi, K. (2016). The effects of childhood maltreatment on brain structure, function and connectivity. *Nature Reviews Neuroscience*, 17, 652–666. doi:10.1038/nrn.2016.111.

Tottenham, N., Hare, T.A., Millner, A., Gilhooly, T., Zevin, J.D. & Casey, B.J. (2011). Elevated amygdala response to faces following early deprivation. *Developmental Science*, 14(2), 190–204. doi:10.1111/j.1467-7687.2010.00971.x.

Tulving, E. (2001). Episodic memory and common sense: How far apart? *Philosophical Transactions of the Royal Society B: Biological Sciences*, 356(1413), 1505–1515. doi:10.1098/rstb.2001.0937.

Tulving, E. (2002). Episodic memory: From mind to brain. *Annual Review of Psychology*, 53(1), 1–25. doi:10.1146/annurev.psych.53.100901.135114.

Wang, J. et al. (2015). Determination of the posterior boundary of Wernicke's area based on multimodal connectivity profiles. *Human Brain Mapping*, 36(5), 1908–1924. doi:10.1002/HBM.22745.

Weissman, D.H., Gopalakrishnan, A., Hazlett, C.J. & Woldorff, M.G. (2005). Dorsal anterior cingulate cortex resolves conflict from distracting stimuli by boosting attention toward relevant events. *Cerebral Cortex*, 15(2), 229–237. doi:10.1093/cercor/bhh125.

Index

For Product Safety Concerns and Information please contact our EU
representative GPSR@taylorandfrancis.com Taylor & Francis Verlag GmbH,
Kaufingerstraße 24, 80331 München, Germany

Printed and bound by CPI Group (UK) Ltd, Croydon, CR0 4YY
08/06/2025
01897005-0018